Chemistry
for students and parents

Key Chemistry Concepts,

Problems and Solutions

Roy Richard Sawyer

Roy Richard Sawyer

ISBN: 9798858237655

Table of Contents

Introduction

My grandma used to bake cakes.
To bake a cake for five people, you have to mix:
I cup of flour
3 eggs
1/2 cup of sugar
100 grams of butter
There was no such thing as fat-free cakes at that time. That is why they tasted so good. :)
What if you need to bake a cake for 20 people? She had the common sense to calculate proportions.
20 is 4 times greater than 5.
So, you must use 4 times the number of cups of flour, 4 times as many number eggs, and so on. As a result, you will have a new recipe.
I * 4=4 cups of flour
3 * 4=12 eggs
1/2 * 4 = 2 cups of sugar
100 * 4 = 400 grams of butter.
In the same way you can solve a problem about a chemical reaction.
All chemical reactions occur in equivalent proportions.
If 10 grams of Na_2CO_3 react with $CaCl_2$, how many grams of $CaCO_3$ is produced?

10g   ? g
$Na_2CO_3 + CaCl_2 = CaCO_3 + 2NaCl$

All compounds react with each other in certain proportions. In a given reaction, one mole of Na_2CO_3 produces one mole of $CaCO_3$.
Mole is molecular mass (MW) in grams.
The atomic mass of $Na = 23$
The atomic mass of $C = 12$
The atomic mass of $O = 16$
For Na_2CO_3 the MW is $23 *2 + 12 + 16*3 = 106$ g. - I mole
For $CaCO_3$ the MW is $40 + 12 + 48 = 100$g. I mole.
106 g Na_2CO_3 produces 100g $CaCO_3$.
10 g Na_2CO_3 produces X g $CaCO_3$.

To calculate X, multiply the matched-up values on the opposite ends of the diagonal and divide the product by the unmatched value, as shown in the figure below.

X=10 * 100 / 106 = 9.4 g of CaCO3

Now you have solved the chemical equation problem and proved to yourself that you can understand chemistry.

The Periodic table

In 1869, Russian chemist Dmitry Mendeleev published an article in which he presented his periodic table of chemical elements. He noticed a repetition of chemical elements' physical and chemical properties when he arranged them according to their atomic weight.

Later, it was proved that elements' physical and chemical properties depend on their number of protons. Since the number of protons determines an element's atomic weight, the elements could be arranged according to their atomic weight. You can find the periodic table on Google.com.

Print the periodic table and have it in front of you while we discuss details.

A two-dimensional periodic table has vertical groups and horizontal periods.

Elements that belong to the same group have similar properties. For example, Sodium (Na) and Potassium (K) are alkaline metals. They belong to the first group. These metals are so soft that they can be cut with a knife. When a small bit of sodium is placed in water, it dissolves, producing a colorless and odorless gas. This gas is hydrogen.

In reaction with water, alkaline metals produce alkali, a strong base. Sodium and water produce Sodium hydroxide. (NaOH)

Sodium belongs to the first group and the third period.

In the 7th group of the same period, we find chlorine Cl. Chlorine is a greenish poisonous gas used as a chemical weapon in WWI. The reaction of mixing chlorine with water produces a strong hydrochloric acid (HCl) Table salt will be produced if you mix sodium hydroxide and hydrochloric acid.

Knowing to which group and period an element belongs, a chemist can tell a lot about the element's properties.

An atom contains three types of particles: positive protons, neutral neutrons, and negative electrons. Protons and neutrons comprise the atomic nucleus, while electrons are located at some distance from the nucleus.

The electron's position in the atom is described by its four quantum numbers: shell, sub-shell, orbital, and spin.

Shells or the main quantum number n can equal any whole number 1, 2, 3... It determines the electron energy and its average distance from the nucleus.

Subshell or angular momentum quantum number l (small L) describes the shape of an electron orbital.

When l=0, the electron's orbital has a spherical shape that is called an S orbital

When l=1, the electron's orbital has a dumbbell shape called a p orbital.

When l=2, the electron's orbital is called a d orbital.

When l=3, the electron's orbital is called an f orbital.

m is a magnetic quantum number. It may change from +l (small L) to -l (small L).

As a result, there are three types of p orbitals (m=-1, m=0, and m=+1). Two electrons may exist on each type of p orbital. In total, 3p orbitals may have 6 electrons.

There are five types of d orbitals (m=-2, m=-1, m=0, m=1, m=2), and two electrons may exist on each type of d orbital. In total, 5d orbitals may have 10 electrons.

There are seven types of f orbitals (m=-3, m=-2, m=-1, m=0, m=1, m=2, m=3), and two electrons may exist on each type of f orbital. In total, 7f orbitals may have 14 electrons.

s - spin projection quantum number or spin of an electron can be $+1/2$ or $-1/2$.

Imagine that you have a desk with a stack of bookshelves. If you have only one book, you will put it on the first shelf. You will not put it on the top shelf near the ceiling. If you have a few books, you put them where it would be easier to reach one. In an atom, the electrons start filling orbitals with the orbital with the lowest energy if it does not contradict the Pauli Exclusion Principle.

The Pauli Exclusion Principle states that no 2 electrons in the same atom may have the same quantum numbers. For example, 2 electrons on the 1S orbital in the helium atom have opposite spins.

When the 1S orbital is filled, the 2S orbital will fill next.

The electronic configuration of a Hydrogen atom is:

H: $1s^1$

It means that hydrogen has only one electron on the first S orbital.

The electronic configuration of the Helium (He) atom is:

He $1s^2$

It means that Helium has two electrons on the first S orbital.

For a He atom, n quantum number $=1$, l (small L) quantum number $= 0$. There is no p orbital for $l=0$. S orbital is filled. Helium cannot have more than 2 electrons on the 1S orbital. As a result, it is a noble gas. Helium cannot form bound with any other elements.

The next element in the periodic table is Lithium (Li). Li starts the second period and has order number 3. It means that it has 3 protons and 3 electrons. Its electronic configuration is:

Li: $1s\ 2\ 2s\ 1$

The next element, Beryllium (Be) has the order number of 4, and it has 2 electrons on the 1S orbital and 2 electrons on the 2S orbital. Two S orbitals are filled for Beryllium. You may wonder why Beryllium is not a noble element if it has filled its S orbitals. The answer is that the completed number of electrons on the second shell is 8 (2 S and 6 P electrons). For Beryllium, the quantum number $n=2$ and the quantum number $l=1$. As a result, an additional p orbital appears for $n=2$. This orbital is not filled for Beryllium.

The Beryllium electronic configuration is:

Be: $1s^2\ 2s^2$

The next element is Boron (B). It has 5 electrons: 2 electrons on the 1S orbital, 2 electrons on the 2S orbital, and 1 electron on the 2P orbital. Filling of the P orbital starts from Boron. Boron electronic configuration is:

B: $1s^2\ 2s^2\ 2p^1$

The following five elements have the outmost electrons on the P orbital, and the number of P electrons is incremented by one for each consequential element.

C: $1s^2\ 2s^2\ 2p^2$

N: $1s^2\ 2s^2\ 2p^3$

O: $1s^2\ 2s^2\ 2p^4$

F: $1s^2\ 2s^2\ 2p^5$

Ne: $1s^2\ 2s^2\ 2p^6$

Neon (Ne) has 6 P electrons. The P orbital is completely filled for Neon. As a result, Neon is a noble gas.

The next element is Sodium (Na). Na's order number is 11. It has the same electronic configuration as Neon plus the 3S orbital. The Sodium electronic configuration can be written in short form as [Ne] $3s^1$ or in long form:

Na: $1s^2\ 2s^2\ 2p^6\ 3s^1$

The next element is Magnesium (Mg). Mg has 2 electrons on the 3S orbital.

Mg: $1s^2\ 2s^2\ 2p^6\ 3s^2$

The next element is Aluminum, which has 1 electron on the 3P orbital. Again, the filing of the P orbital starts from Al, and for the following five elements, the number of P electrons is incremented by one for each consequential element.

Argon (Ar), a noble gas, has the complete set of 6 electrons on the 3P orbital.

Al: $1s^2\ 2s^2\ 2p^6\ 3s^2\ 3p^1$

Si: $1s^2\ 2s^2\ 2p^6\ 3s^2\ 3p^2$

P: $1s^2\ 2s^2\ 2p^6\ 3s^2\ 3p^3$

S: $1s^2\ 2s^2\ 2p^6\ 3s^2\ 3p^4$

Cl: $1s^2\ 2s^2\ 2p^6\ 3s^2\ 3p^5$

Ar: $1s^2\ 2s^2\ 2p^6\ 3s^2\ 3p^6$

Argon's main quantum number, n, is 3, and l is 2. Remember, we pointed out earlier that when l=2 additional d orbital appeared. So, we may expect the next element, Potassium, to have the outmost electron on the 3d orbital. Potassium has one of the outmost electrons on the 4S orbital. The 4S orbital has a lower energy than the 3d orbital, so the 4S orbital is filled before the 3d orbital.

K: $1s^2\ 2s^2\ 2p^6\ 3s^2\ 3p^6\ 4s^1$

The next element, Calcium (Ca) has 2 electrons on the 4S orbital.

Ca: $1s^2\ 2s^2\ 2p^6\ 3s^2\ 3p^6\ 4s^2$

The 3d orbital starts filling from Scandium (Sc). Then, until Gallium (Ga), the d orbital is filling.

Sc: $1s^2\ 2s^2\ 2p^6\ 3s^2\ 3p^6\ 4s^2\ 3d^1$

Ti: $1s^2\ 2s^2\ 2p^6\ 3s^2\ 3p^6\ 4s^2\ 3d^2$

V: $1s^2\ 2s^2\ 2p^6\ 3s^2\ 3p^6\ 4s^2\ 3d^3$

Cr: $1s^2\ 2s^2\ 2p^6\ 3s^2\ 3p^6\ 4s^1\ 3d^5$

Mn: $1s^2\ 2s^2\ 2p^6\ 3s^2\ 3p^6\ 4s^2\ 3d^5$

Fe: $1s^2\ 2s^2\ 2p^6\ 3s^2\ 3p^6\ 4s^2\ 3d^6$

Co: $1s^2\ 2s^2\ 2p^6\ 3s^2\ 3p^6\ 4s^2\ 3d^7$

Ni: $1s^2\ 2s^2\ 2p^6\ 3s^2\ 3p^6\ 4s^2\ 3d^8$

Cu: $1s^2\ 2s^2\ 2p^6\ 3s^2\ 3p^6\ 4s^1\ 3d^{10}$

Zn: $1s^2\ 2s^2\ 2p^6\ 3s^2\ 3p^6\ 4s^2\ 3d^{10}$

Ga: $1s^2\ 2s^2\ 2p^6\ 3s^2\ 3p^6\ 4s^2\ 3d^{10}\ 4p^1$

Interestingly, Vanadium has $3d^3\ 4S^2$ electrons, and the next element, Chromium (Cr), should have $3d^4\ 4S^2$ electrons, but it has $3d^5 4S^1$ electrons. One electron passed from the 4S orbital to the 3d orbital.

Nickel has 8 electrons on the d orbital. The next element, Copper (Cu), should have 9 electrons on the 3d orbital and 2 electrons on the 4S orbital, but actually Copper has ten electrons on the 3d orbital and one on the 4S orbital. One electron passed from the 4S orbital to the 3d orbital. The electronic configuration of copper is $[Ar]\ 3d^{10}4S^1$.

The complete list of electronic configurations of all the chemical elements can be found in Wikipedia:

http://en.wikipedia.org/wiki/Electron_configurations_of_the_l ements_%28data_page%29

All elements can be divided into metals and nonmetals.

Metals are on the left, and nonmetals are on the right in the periodic table.

The group number shows how many electrons are in the outermost orbital. These electrons are called valence electrons. For example, Na (sodium) is in the first group. It has one electron on the outermost orbital. Na can easily give this electron to Cl (chlorine). Cl is in the seventh group. It has 7 electrons, and it takes one electron from Na. As a result, Na becomes a positive ion – (Na+), and Cl becomes a negative ion – (Cl -). Ions with opposite charges form ionic bonds.

Ionic bonds usually form crystal structures. That is why salt is made of crystals.

Carbon C is in the 4th group. It has four valence electrons. As a result, C forms four covalent bonds with four atoms of Cl.

C does not give its electrons to Cl. Carbon and chlorine share electrons. When atoms share electrons, they form covalent bonds.

Oxides

Oxides are produced when metals or nonmetals react with oxygen. Oxygen is in the 6th group and has six valence electrons. It tends to gain two more electrons to become a complete octet, and its valence is 2.

$2Ca + O_2 = 2CaO$

In nature, metal oxides exist in clay. Clay is a mixture of oxides.

SiO_2

Al_2O_3

K_2O

Na_2O

MgO

CaO

Fe_2O_3

TiO_2

Bases

In reaction with water, metals or metal oxides produce a base:

$2Na + 2H2O = 2NaOH + H2$

$CaO + H2O = Ca(OH)2$

Bases dissociate in water and produce a negative hydroxide OH - ion.

Acids

Nonmetal oxides are NO2, SO3, P2O5

In reaction with water, nonmetal oxides produce acids:

$H2O + SO3 = H2SO4$ - sulfuric acid

$H2O + NO2 = HNO3$ - nitric acid

$H2O + CO2 = H2CO3$ - Carbonic acid

Acids dissociate in water and produce proton of hydrogen H+.

Salts

When an acid reacts with a base, salt is produced.

$NaOH + HNO3 = NaNO3 + H2O$

To calculate the percentage composition of NaNO3, find the molecular mass of NaNO3.

23 (Na) + 12 (N) + 16*3 (O3) = 83

The molecular weight of NaNO3 = 83

83 - 100%

23 (Na) - X%

X = 23 * 100 /83 = 27.7% of Na

83 - 100%

12 (N) - X %

X = 12 * 100/83 = 14.5% of N

83 - 100%

48 (O) - X %

X = 48 * 100/83 = 57.8 % of O

Some salts are more soluble in water; some are less, some are insoluble.

When an acid and base reaction produces an insoluble salt, it precipitates.

$Ca(OH)2 + H2CO3 = CaCO3 + 2H2O$

CaCO3 is insoluble in water and forms a white precipitate.

Salts may react with each other and produce new salts.

For example, $BaCl_2 + Na_2SO_4 = BaSO_4 + 2NaCl$

$BaSO_4$ is insoluble and precipitates.

Equivalent proportions

All chemical reactions occur in equivalent proportions.

1. How many grams of Ca Cl2 is spent in the following reaction:

10g   ? g

$Na_2CO_3 + Ca\ Cl_2 = CaCO_3 + 2NaCl$

All compounds react with each other in certain proportions.

In a given reaction, one mole of Na_2CO_3 reacts with one mole of $CaCl_2$.

A mole is MW (molecular mass) in grams.

For Na_2CO_3 MW is $23\ ^*2 + 12 + 48 = 106$ g. $= 1$ mole

For $CaCl_2$ MW is $40 + 35^*2 = 110$g. $= 1$ mole.

106 g Na_2CO_3 reacts with 110g $CaCl_2$.

10g Na_2CO_3 reacts with X g $CaCl_2$.

$X = 10\ ^*\ 110 / 106 = 10.38$ g $CaCl_2$

2. How many grams of $CaCO_3$ is produced if 100 ml of 0.5 M solution of Na_2CO_3 reacts with an unlimited volume of solution $CaCl_2$?

0.5 M

2. $Na_2CO_3 + Ca\ Cl_2 = CaCO_3 + 2\ NaCl$

100 ml

1 liter of 1 M solution of Na_2CO_3 contains 106 g

How many grams of Na_2CO_3 are in 1 liter of 0.5 M solution?

1 M - 106 g

0.5 M - X g

$X = 0.5\ M\ ^*\ 106\ g / 1\ M = 53$ g

A liter of 0.5 M solution contains 53 grams of Na_2CO_3.

How many grams of Na_2CO_3 are in 100 ml?

1 liter - 53 g

0.1 liter - X g

$X = 0.1\ ^*\ 53 / 1 = 5.3$ g

106 g of Na_2CO_3 produces 100 g of $CaCO_3$.

5.3 g of Na_2CO_3 produces X g of $CaCO_3$.

X= 5.3 * 100 / 106 = 5 g

Acid-Base reactions

Molarity vs. Molality vs. Normality

What is Molarity?

What is Molality?

What is Normality?

Molar solution is a concentration of solution, one liter of which contains a mass of solute in grams equal to the molecular mass of solute.

A solute is a substance which is dissolved in another substance.

A solvent is a substance that dissolves a solute.

1. Let's say we have 100 ml of H_2SO_4 solution, and it contains 0.49 g of H_2SO_4

MW of $H_2SO_4 = 2 + 32 + 4* 16 = 98g$

1 mole $= 98g/L$

We must find how many grams of H_2SO_4 given solution are contained in 1 liter.

100 ml $= 0.1$ L and contains 0.49 g

1 L contains X g

X $= 0.49 * 1 / 0.1 = 4.9$ g.

98g/L - 1 mole

4.9 g/L - X mole

X $= 4.9 * 1 / 98 = 0.05$ mole

The molarity of a 100 ml solution of H_2SO_4, which contains 0.49 g of H_2SO_4, equals 0.05 mole.

What is Molality? Molality is moles of solute/kg of solvent.

What is normality? An equivalent is the molecular mass or mass of acid or base that produces one mole of protons (H+) or one mole of hydroxyl (OH-) ions.

One mole of H_2SO_4 produces 2 moles of H+ then equivalent to

$H_2SO_4 = MW/2 = 49g/L$

49g/L is 1 Normal solution.

4.9g/L solution is - X N

X= 4.9 * 1/ 49 = 0.10 N.

The normality of 100 ml solution of H2SO4, which contains 0.49 g of H2SO4, equals 0.10 N.

2. We have 10 ml of NaOH of unknown concentration. The solution was titrated with 0.10 N solution of H2SO4, and 15 ml was required for neutralization. What is the concentration of NaOH?

Nb * Vb = Na * Va

where V is volume, N is Normality, b - base, and a - acid

Nb = Na * Va / Vb = 0.10 * 15 / 10 = 0.15 N

The concentration of NaOH = 0.15 N.

Weight and Volume problems:

1. How many liters of hydrogen are produced from one liter of water?

2H20 = 2H2 + 02

First, we must find how many grams of water are spent and how many grams of H2 are produced.

MW of H20 = 2 + 16 = 18

If we spent two molecules of H20, then we spent 18 * 2 =36 g.

MW H2 = 2, and we got two molecules of H2. 2*2 = 4g.

36 g of water produces 4 g of Hydrogen.

1000 g of water produces X g of hydrogen.

X = 4 * 100 / 36 = 111.1 g

One mole of gas under normal conditions occupies 22.4 liters.

So, we have to know how many moles of H2 are produced.

1 mole of H2 equals 2 g.

X mole of H2 equals 111.1g.

X = 111.1g / 2g = 50.6 moles of H2.

1 mole of H2 occupies 22.4 liters.

50.6 moles of H2 occupy X liters.

X = 50.6 moles * 22.4L = 1232 L.

Equilibrium. Le Chatelier's Principle

Any chemical reaction goes both ways.

According to Le Chatelier, if, at the equilibrium point, we make any change in concentration, pressure, or temperature, the equilibrium point will move to counteract the change.

If the reaction produces heat, heating the system will move the equilibrium to the left, and cooling the system will shift the balance to the right. If the volume of the products is greater than the volume of the reactants, then increasing the pressure will move the equilibrium to the left. Decreasing the pressure will shift the equilibrium to the right. Increasing the concentration of reactants will move the equilibrium to the right, and increasing the concentration of the products will move the equilibrium to the left. For a reaction $A + B = C + D$, the Equilibrium constant

$$K_c = [C] * [D] / [A] * [B]$$

where [ ] is the concentration in moles.

$$H2 + I2 <=> 2HI$$

The concentration of products and reactants is raised to the power of their respective coefficients.

$$K_c = [HI]^2 / [H2][I2]$$

The concentration of products and reactants is raised to the power of their respective coefficients: a, b, c, and d.

Let us calculate the equilibrium constant for the following reaction.

$$2Al + 6HCl + H20 = 2AlCl3 + 3H2$$

The concentration of HCl is 0,5 M, the concentration of $AlCl3$ is 0.2M, and the concentration of H2 is 0.2M at the equilibrium point.

What is the equilibrium constant?

$$Kc = ([0.2]^2 * [0.2]^3) / [0.5]^6$$

$$Kc = 0.04 * 0.008/0.015625$$

$$Kc = 0.00032/0.015625 = 0.02048$$

If all reaction components are gases, partial pressure is used to calculate the equivalent constant instead of concentration. To understand the partial pressure of a gas, imagine that we have a closed container with an air pressure of 10 atmospheres. Let us say that the air contains 75% Nitrogen, 23% Oxygen, 1% CO2, and 1% Argon.

What is the partial pressure of each gas?

The the partial pressure of N2 will be 0.75 * 10 atm =7.5 atm

The partial pressure of O2 will be 0.23* 10 atm=2.3 atm

The partial pressure of CO2 will be 0.01 * 10atm=0.1 atm

The partial pressure of Ar will be 0.01 * 10 atm=0.1 atm

The sum of all mixed gases' partial pressures will equal the total air pressure.

7.5 atm + 2.3 atm + 0.1 atm + 0.1 atm=10 atm

Kp = PD^d * PC^c / PA^a * PB^b

Where PA, PB, PC, and PD are the partial pressures in the atmosphere (atm) units and a, b, c, d are coefficients.

Example:

H2(g) + Cl2(g) = 2HCl(g)

The partial pressure of H2 and Cl2 will be 2 atm, and the partial pressure of HCl will be 1atm.

Then Kp=1^2 / 2 * 2= 0.25

Since products of the reaction go to the numerator, and initial reactants go to the denominator, the equilibrium constant is greater when the equilibrium moves to the right.

Let us solve such a problem when the concentration at the equilibrium point is known only for one product and not for the other product or reactant.

N2 + 3H2 = 2NH3

Initially, we had 0.2 moles of N2 and 0.6 moles of H2. At the equivalent point, we had 0.1 moles of N2. Calculate the equilibrium constant.

Let us build an ICE chart. In an ICE chart or table, I stands for initial, C stands for change, and E stands for equilibrium.

You can read in Wikipedia.

http://en.wikipedia.org/wiki/ICE

	[N2]	[H2]	[NH3]
Initial concentration:	0.2M	0.6M	0
Change in concentration -	-X	-3X	+2X
Concentration at Equilibrium	0.1 M	0.3M	0.2M

Let us denote the change in N2 concentration as X, then the change in H2 concentration will be -3X because one mole of N2 reacts with 3 moles of H2. The minus sign shows that the N2 and H2 concentration is decreasing because they produce NH3. The concentration of NH3 will be increased, and the change in NH3 concentration will be +2X because one mole of N2 produces 2 moles of NH3.

Initially, we had 0.2M of N2. At the equilibrium point concentration of N2 was 0.1M.

The change for N2 concentration is 0.2M - 0.1M= 0.1M.

Since the change of N2 is defined as X, X=0.1M, and 3X=0.1*3=0.3M

From the ICE table, we can see that at the equilibrium point, the concentration of H2 becomes 0.6M - 0.3M=0.3M, and the concentration of NH3 becomes 0 + 0.2M = 0.2M

$Kc = 0.2^2 / 0.1 * 0.3^3 = 0.04 / 0.1*0.027 = 0.04/0.0027 = 14.8$

Next problem: $H2 (g) + Cl2(g) = 2HCl(g)$

Given: Initially, we had 1M H2, 3M Cl2, and Kc=0.5 What are concentrations at equilibrium?

Build an ICE table.

	[H2]	[CL2]	[HCl]
Initial concentration	1M	1M	0
Changes in concentration	X	X	+2X
Concentrations at Equilibrium	1-X	1-X	+2X

The change for HCl is 2X because the coefficient for HCl is 2. It means for each mole of spent H2, 2 moles of HCl are produced.
Kc = 2X^2 / (1-X) * X = 0.5
Solve the quadratic equation and find that X=0.2M.
H2 Concentrations at Equilibrium = 1M-0.2M=0.8 M.
Cl2 Concentrations at Equilibrium =1M-0.2M = 0.8M.
HCl Concentrations at Equilibrium =0.2M *2 = 0.4M.

pH Acidity of a solution

The acidity of the solution depends on the concentration of hydrogen ions. For example, hydrochloric acid is produced in the stomach. In the aquatic environment, it dissociates into positive hydrogen ions and negative chlorine ions. Therefore, the environment in the stomach is acidic.
pH = - Log [H+]
Where [H+] is the concentration of H+ ions.

What is log?
Log is a logarithm with base 10.
log 10 = 1 because 10^1 = 10
log100 = 2 because 10^2 = 100.
log 1000 = 3 because 10^3 = 1000
log1/1000 = -3 because 10^ - 3 = 1/1000
- log 1/1000 = 3.
The pH of water is 7 (neutral).
What is the pH of 0.0001 N HCl?
HCl = H+ + Cl -

The concentration of H+ equals the concentration of HCl = 0.0001 N.
pH = - log [1 * 10^ - 4] = 4

Freezing point

Water freezes at 0 C. But if you take a salt solution, it will not freeze at 0
C. The freezing point of the salt solution will be below 0 C. Knowing the
concentration of the solution, you can calculate how much the freezing
point of the solution will decrease.
The freezing point constant = degree C per 1M of solute per 1000g of
solvent.
A solute is a substance dissolved in another substance.
A solvent is a substance in which another substance is dissolved.
For water F pk = 1.86°C kg/mole.
Freezing point depression equals the number of particles into which the
solute dissociated in the solvent multiplied by the solvent's Freezing point
constant multiplied by the solute's number of moles per kilogram of the
solvent.

$$Fpd = i * Fpk * m$$

Where Fpd is Freezing point depression.
i -Van't Hoff factor (the number of solute particles).
Fpk is the Freezing point constant.
m - Molality of the solution.

Since one kilogram of water is the weight of one liter of water, the
Molarity of a water solution is the same as Molality.
1. Given: 1 M of NaCl is dissolved in one kilogram of water.
What is the freezing point?
The Molality of the solution is 1 mole/kg.
The number of particles is 2 (Na+ ion and Cl- ion).

Fpd=2 * 1 mole/kg * 1.86°C kg/mole=3.72C
The freezing point of water is 0 C, then the freezing point of the solution

= 0 C - 3.72 C = -3.72C.

2. Given: 196 g of H2SO4 added to 500 g of water.
What is the freezing point of the solution?
How many moles of H2SO4 are in 196g?
MW = 2+32+64=98g
196g/98g = 2 M.
2M. is 500g.
X M is 1000g.
X = 2 * 1000 / 500 = 4 M.
What is the number of particles?
H2SO4 dissociates in water to form two H+ ions and one SO42-
Fpd=3 * 4 moles/kg *1.86°C kg/mole=22.32C
Frp = 0 C - 22.32C= -22.32 C
Where 0C is the freezing point of water.
The freezing point of depression is -22.32

3. 100 g of glucose C6H12O6 is dissolved in 500 g of water.
What is the freezing point?
Glucose MW = 6*12 + 12*2 + 6*16=180.16g
100 g per 500g
X g per 1000g
X = 100*1000/500 = 200g

180.16g per 1000g -is 1 mole/kg
200 g per 1000 is X mole/kg

Molality of Glucose = 200g * 1 mole/kg/180.16g=1.11 mole/kg

Glucose does not dissociate in water. It means the number of particles is 1.

Fpd=1 * 1.11 mole/kg * 1.86°C kg/mole=2.06C
0C - 2.06C = -2.06C
The freezing point of depression is 2.06C

Boiling Point

Water boils at 100 degrees C. But salt water does not boil at 100 degrees C. For salt water to boil, its temperature must be above 100 degrees C. Knowing the concentration of the solution, you can calculate how much the boiling point of the solution will increase.

$Bp = i * Kb * m$

i - the Van't Hoff factor (the number of solute particles)

Kb is the boiling point constant.

m - Molality of the solution

For water $Kb = 0.52$ °C kg/mole

1. Given: 106 g Na_2CO_3 in 500 g of water. What is the boiling point of the solution?

MW of $Na_2CO_3 = 23+23+12+48 = 106g$.

106 g in 500 g water.

Xg in 1000g water.

$X = 106 * 1000 / 500 = 212$ g.

106 g/L - 1 mole/kg.

212 g/L - X moles/kg.

$X = 212 / 106 = 2$ moles/kg.

Bp. elevation $= 2$ moles/kg $* 0.52$Ckg/mole $= 1.4$ C.

$Bp = 100$ C $+ 1.4$ C $= 101.4$ C.

2. Given: 196 g of H_2SO_4 added to 500 g of water.

What is the boiling point of the solution?

How many moles of H_2SO_4 are in 196g?

$MW = 2+32+64 = 98g$.

$196g/98g = 2$ M.

2M. is 500g.

X M is 1000g.

$X = 2 * 1000 / 500 = 4$ M.

What is the number of particles?

H_2SO_4 dissociates in water to form two H+ ions and one SO_4^{2-}.

Bp elevation $= 3 * 4$moles/kg $*0.52$°C kg/mole $= 6.24$C.

$Bp = 100$ C $+ 6.24$C $= 106.24$ C.

23

Where 100C is the boiling point of water.

The boiling point is 106.24 C.

3. 100 g of glucose C6H12O6 is dissolved in 500 g water.

What is the boiling point?

Glucose MW = 6*12 + 12*2 + 6*16=180.16g

100 g per 500g.

X g per 1000g.

X = 100*1000/500 = 200g.

180.16g per 1000g -is 1 mole/kg.

200 g per 1000 is X moles/kg.

Molality of Glucose = 200g * 1 mole/kg/180.16g=1.11 moles/kg

Glucose does not dissociate in water. It means the number of particles is 1.

Bp elevation=1 * 1.11 mole/kg * 0.52°C kg/mole=0.58C

100C + 0.58C =100.58C

The boiling point is 100.58C

How to Balance Redox Reactions

What is Redox Reaction? In the Redox reaction, one agent loses electrons while another gains electrons. An agent that is losing electrons is oxidized. An agent that is gaining electrons is reduced. Oxidation is losing electrons; Reduction is gaining electrons. How to memorize that?

Oxidation is related to corrosion and rust. When your bicycle is rusted, then you are losing it. It may help you to remember that oxidation is lost. Sometimes it is obvious what is oxidized. For example,

$S + O2 = SO2$ Oxygen is a strong oxidizing agent. Any compound or element that reacts with Oxygen is oxidized. Initially, S was neutral, and in the end, it became S4+. How do we calculate that? SO2 is neutral.

In SO_2, O has a charge of -2. Two O have a charge of -4. Then to make SO_2 neutral, S must have a charge of +4.

$X + 2(-2) = 0$

$X - 4 = 0$

$X = +4$.

Sometimes it is not obvious what is oxidized and what is reduced.

$H_2S + FeCl_3 = S + FeCl_2 + HCl$

In the reaction above, in H_2S, sulfur has a charge of -2. How do we get it?

Hydrogen usually has a charge of +1.

In H_2S, we have two hydrogen atoms, and their charge is +2. H_2S is neutral.

It means that S has charge 2. At the end of the reaction, sulfur becomes neutral.

It is losing 2 electrons.

$S^{2-} - 2e = S$

Fe in $FeCl_3$ has a charge of +3. At the end of the reaction, it becomes Fe^{2+}. It is gaining one electron.

$Fe^{3+} + 1e = Fe^{2+}$

What is oxidized, and what is reduced? Sulfur is oxidized because it loses electrons, and Fe is reduced by gaining electrons.

Let us try to balance Redox reactions.

1. NaNO3 = NaNO2 + O2

Let us write half of the reaction of the oxidation and Reduction. Initially, Nitrogen has a charge of +5, and at the end of the reaction, it has a charge of +3.

How do we calculate that?

In $NaNO_3$, Oxygen has a charge of -2. Sodium has a charge of +1. The molecule of $NaNO_3$ is neutral. It means that negative charges inside the $NaNO_3$ molecule must equal positive charges.

$Na (+1) + O_3 (-2 \times 3) = 1 - 6 = -5$.

Then Nitrogen has to be + 5 to make the molecule neutral.

In $NaNO_2$, Nitrogen has a charge of +3. Nitrogen must receive two negative electrons to change its charge from +5 to +3.

$5 + (-2) = 3$

So, we can write:

N5+ + 2e = N3+ | 2

Oxygen initially has a charge of -2.

At the end of the reaction, it becomes neutral and has a charge of 0.

So, we can write:

2O2- - 4e = O2 | 4

Combine two half-reactions and get:

N5+ + 2e = N3+ | 2

2O2- - 4e = O2 | 4

Since 2 and 4 can be divided by 2, we get 1 and 2

N5+ + 2e = N3+ | 2 1

2O2- - 4e = O2 | 4 2

Now switch positions of 1 and 2:

N5+ + 2e = N3+ | 2 1 2

2O2- - 4e = O2 | 4 2 1

From the above, N5+ and N3+ should have a coefficient of 2.

Oxygen should have a coefficient of 1.

2NaNO3 = 2NaNO2 + O2

Check the equation balance: from both sides of the equation. We have 2 Na, 2 N, and 6 O.

We are done.

The strongest oxidizing element is fluorine. It is stronger than Oxygen. As a result, in F2O, Oxygen has a charge of +2. It is very unusual for Oxygen. We know that usually, it has a charge of -2. In H2O2, Oxygen also has an unusual charge of -1.

Chlorine is the third oxidizing agent after Oxygen. Usually, it has a charge of -1, but compounds with Oxygen may have a positive charge.

For example, in KClO3, chlorine has a charge of +5.

K has a charge of +1, and O has a charge of -2. KClO3 is neutral.

The sum of all charges of KClO3 equals 0.

$X + 1 + (3 * -2) = 0$ Then

$X - 5 = 0$

$X = +5.$

Chlorine has a charge of +5.

Try to balance the following equations by yourself.
Detailed answers are included.

2. $Fe + H_2SO_4 = FeSO_4 + H_2$

3. $NO_2 + H_2O = HNO_3 + HNO_2$

4. $Fe S_2 + HNO_3 \rightarrow Fe (NO_3)_3 + H_2SO_4 + NO_2$

5. $HgO = Hg + O_2$

6. $AgNO_3 + H_2O = Ag + HNO_3 + O_2$

7. $Fe_2O_3 + H_2 = Fe + H_2O$

8. $H_2O = H_2 + O_2$

9. $Fe_2O_3 + CO = Fe + CO_2$

10. $KClO_3 = KCl + O_2$

11. $H_2O_2 = H_2O + O_2$

12. $HBr + H_2O_2 = Br_2 + H_2O$

13. $MnCO_3 + KClO_3 = MnO_2 + KCl + CO_2$

14. $H_2S + SO_2 = S + H_2O$

15. $Sb + HNO_3 = HSbO_3 + NO_2 + H_2O$

16. $Al + CuCl_2 = AlCl_3 + Cu$

17. $Zn + CuSO_4 = ZnSO_4 + Cu$

18. $MnS + HClO_3 = MnSO_4 + HCl;$

19. $H_2S + FeCl_3 = S + FeCl_2 + HCl$

20. $CuO + CO = Cu + CO_2$

21. $Bi + HNO_3 = Bi(NO_3)_3 + NO_2 + H_2O$

22. $PbS + HNO_3 = PbSO_4 + NO_2 + H_2O$

23. $C + HNO_3 = CO_2 + NO_2 + H_2O$

24. $FeSO_4 + Br_2 + H_2SO_4 = Fe_2(SO_4)_3 + HBr$

25. $Al + HCl = AlCl_3 + H_2$

26. $KMnO_4 + SO_2 + H_2O = MnSO_4 + H_2SO_4 + K_2SO_4$

27. $MnO_2 + HCl = MnCl_2 + H_2O + Cl_2$

28. $Cl_2 + KOH = KCl + KClO_3 + H_2O$

29. $KMnO_4 + NH_3 = MnO_2 + KOH + N_2 + H_2O$

30. $Mg + HNO_3 = Mg(NO_3)_2 + NH_4NO_3 + H_2O$

Answers

2. $Fe + H_2SO_4 = FeSO_4 + H_2\uparrow$

Fe initially is neutral, and at the end, it becomes +2. It means that Fe lost 2 electrons.

$Fe - 2e = Fe^{2+} \mid 2$

Hydrogen has a charge of +1 in H_2SO_4, and it becomes neutral at the end.

$2H^+ + 2e = H_2 \mid 2$

Combine two half-reactions and get:

$Fe - 2e = Fe^{2+} \mid 2$

$2H^+ + 2e = H_2 \mid 2$

Since 2 = 2, the equation is already balanced:

$Fe + H_2SO_4 = FeSO_4 + H_2 \uparrow$

3. NO2 + H2O = HNO3 + HNO2

In NO_2, Nitrogen has a charge of +4. In HNO_3, Nitrogen has a charge of +5

From NO_2, Nitrogen oxidizes to HNO_3.

$N^{4+} - e = N^{5+} \mid 1$

Also, from NO_2, Nitrogen reduces to HNO_2. In NO_2, Nitrogen has a charge of 4+, and in HNO_2, Nitrogen has a charge of 3+.

$N^{4+} + 1e = N^{3+} \mid 1$

Combine two half-reactions and get:

$N^{4+} - 1e = N^{5+} \mid 1$

$N^{4+} + 1e = N^{3+} \mid 1$

Since 1 = 1, we should not have any coefficients, but we have to note that the same N^{4+} is used in both half-reactions, so we have to put 2 in front of it.

$2NO_2 + H_2O = HNO_3 + HNO_2$.

Check the balance: On both sides, we have 2 N, 5 O, and 2 H. We are done.

4. FeS2 + HNO3 → Fe(NO3)3 + H2SO4 + NO2

Fe has a charge of +2 in FeS_2 and +3 in $Fe(NO_3)_3$. Why?

Fe ions may have a charge of +3 or +2.

In FeS_2, it cannot have a charge of +3 because then S would have a charge of -1.5.

It is not possible.

So, Fe in FeS_2 has a charge of 2+, and S has a charge of -1.

NO_3 ion always has a charge of -1.

That is why Fe in $Fe(NO_3)_3$ has a charge of +3.

$Fe2+ - 1e = Fe3+ \mid 1$

Sulfur has a charge of -1 in FeS_2 and a charge of +6 in H_2SO_4 (because O has a charge of -2 and H has a charge of +1)

$+1 \times 2 + 4 \times (-2) = 2 - 8 = -6$.

To make the H_2SO_4 molecule neutral, S should have a charge of + 6.

$S1- - 7e = S6+ \mid 7$

Nitrogen in HNO_3 has a charge of +5, and in NO_2, it has a charge of +4.

$N5+ + 1e = N4+ \mid 1$

Combine three half-reactions and get:

$Fe2+ - 1e = Fe3+ \mid 1$

$2S1- - 14e = 2S6+ \mid 14$

$N5+ + 1e = N4+ \mid 1$

If Fe and S give 15 electrons, then Nitrogen should receive 15 electrons.

$Fe2+ + 2S1- -15e = Fe3+ + 2S6+ \mid 15\ 1$

$N5+ + 1e = N4+ \mid 1\ 15$

That is why we have to put 15 in front of HNO_3.

$FeS_2 + 15HNO_3 \rightarrow Fe(NO_3)_3 + H_2SO_4 + 15NO_2$

Note that not all ions of NO_3 produce NO_2. 3 ions of NO_3 remain as they are in $Fe(NO_3)_3$

So, we have to add three more HNO_3 and get $18HNO_3$.

$FeS_2 + 18HNO_3 = Fe(NO_3)_3 + 2H_2SO_4 + 15NO_2 + H_2O$

Now to balance H and O, add H_2O to the right side of the equation and get:

$FeS_2 + 18HNO_3 = Fe(NO_3)_3 + 2H_2SO_4 + 15NO_2 + 7H_2O$.

We are done. It was a hard one!

5. HgO = Hg + O2 ↑

$Hg^{2+} + 2e = Hg \mid 2\ I\ 2$
$2O_2 - -4e = O_2 \mid 4\ 2\ I$

$2HgO = 2Hg + O_2 \uparrow$

6. $AgNO_3 + H_2O = Ag\downarrow + HNO_3 + O_2\uparrow$

$Ag^{I+} + Ie = Ag \mid I\ 4$
$2O_2 - - 4e = O_2 \mid 4\ I$

$4AgNO_3 + 2H_2O = 4Ag\downarrow + 4HNO_3 + O_2\uparrow$

7. $Fe_2O_3 + H_2 = Fe + H_2O$

$Fe^{3+} + 3e = Fe \mid 3\ 2$
$H_2 - 2e = 2H^+ \mid 2\ 3$

$2F_2O_3 + 6H_2 = 2Fe + 6H_2O$

8. $H_2O = H_2 + O_2$

$2H^+ + 2e = H_2 \mid 2\ I\ 2$
$2O_2 - - 4e = O_2 \mid 4\ 2\ I$

$2H_2O = 2H_2 + O_2$

9. $Fe_2O_3 + CO = Fe + CO_2$

$2Fe^{3+} + 6e = 2Fe \mid 6\ 3\ I$
$C^{2+} - 2e = C^{4+} \mid 2\ I\ 3$

Fe2O3 + 3CO = 2Fe + 3CO2

10. KClO3 = KCl + O2

Cl5+ + 6e = Cl- |6 3 2
2O2- - 4e = O2 |4 2 3

2KClO3 = 2KCl + 3O2

11. H2O2 = H2O + O2

O- + 1e = O2- |1 2
2O - - 2e = O2 |2 1

2H2O2 = 2H2O + O2

12. HBr+ H2O2= Br2 + H2O

2Br- -2e = Br2 |2 1
O- +1e = O2- |1 2

2HBr + H2O2= Br2 + 2H2O

13. MnCO3 + KClO3 = MnO2 + KCl + CO2

Mn2+ - 2 e = Mn4+ |2 1 3
Cl5+ + 6e = Cl- |6 3 1

3MnCO3 + KClO3 = 3MnO2 + KCl + 3CO2

14. H2S + SO2 = S + H2O

$S2- - 2e = S \mid 2\ 2\ 1$
$S4+ +4e = S \mid 4\ 1\ 2$

$2H2S + SO2 = 3S + 2H2O$

15. Sb+HNO3=HSbO3 + NO2 + H2O

$Sb - 5e = Sb5+ \mid 5\ 1$
$N5+ - 1e = N4+ \mid 1\ 5$

$Sb + 5HNO3 = HSbO3 + 5NO2 + 2H2O$

16. Al + CuCl2 = AlCl3 + Cu.

$Al - 3e = Al3+ \mid 3\ 2$
$Cu2+ + 2e = Cu \mid 2\ 3$

$2Al + 3CuCl2 = 2AlCl3 + 3Cu.$

17. Zn + CuSO4 = ZnSO4 + Cu

$Zn - 2e = Zn2+ \mid 2\ 1$
$Cu2+ + 2e = Cu \mid 2\ 1$

.

The equation is balanced.

18. MnS + HClO3 = MnSO4 +HCl;

$S2- - 8e = S6+ \mid 8\ 4\ 3$
$Cl5+ + 6e = Cl- \mid 6\ 3\ 4$

$3MnS + 4HClO_3 = 3MnSO_4 + 4HCl.$

19. H2S + FeCl3 = S + FeCl2 + HCl

$S_{2-} - 2e = S \mid 2 \ 1$
$Fe_{3+} + 1e = Fe_{2+} \mid 1 \ 2$

$H_2S + 2FeCl_3 = S + 2FeCl_2 + 2HCl$

20. CuO + CO = Cu + CO2

$Cu_{2+} + 2e = Cu \mid 2 \ 1$
$C_{2+} - 2e = C_{4+} \mid 2 \ 1$
The equation is balanced.

21. Bi+HNO3=Bi(NO3)3 + NO2 + H2O

$Bi - 3e = Bi_{3+} \mid 3 \ 1$
$N_{5+} + 1e = N_{4+} \mid 1 \ 3$

Since 3 NO_3 are spent to produce $Bi(NO_3)_3$ and 3 NO_3 are required to produce 3 electrons, we have to put 6 in front of HNO_3, not 3.

$Bi + 6HNO_3 = Bi(NO_3)_3 + 3NO_2 + 3H_2O$

22. PbS + HNO3 = PbSO4 + NO2 + H2O

$S_{2-} - 8e = S_{6+} \mid 8 \ 1$
$N_{5+} - 1e = N_{4+} \mid 1 \ 8$

$PbS + 8HNO_3 = PbSO_4 + 8NO_2 + 4H_2O$

23. C+ HNO3=CO2 + NO2 + H2O

$C - 4e = C4+ \quad | \; 4 \; 1$
$N5+ +1e = N4+ \quad | \; 1 \; 4$

$C + 4HNO3 = CO2 + 4NO2 + 2H2O$

24. FeSO4 + Br2 + H2SO4= Fe2(SO4)3 + HBr

$Fe2+ - 1e = Fe3+ \quad | \; 1 \; 2$
$Br2 + 2e = 2Br- \quad | \; 2 \; 1$

$2FeSO4 + Br2 + H2SO4= Fe2(SO4)3+2HBr$

25. Al + HCl = AlCl3 + H2

$Al - 3e = Al3+ \quad | \; 3 \; 2$
$2H+ + 2e = H2 \quad | \; 2 \; 3$

$2Al + 6HCl = 2AlCl3 + 3H2$

We have 6 in front of HCL because (2H+) * 3 = 6

26. KMnO4 + SO2 + H2O = MnSO4 + H2SO4 + K2SO4

$Mn7+ + 5e = Mn2+ \quad | \; 5 \; 2$
$S4+ - 2e = S6+ \quad | \; 2 \; 5$

$2KMnO4 + 5SO2 + 2H2O = 2MnSO4 + 2H2SO4 + K2SO4$

27. MnO2 + HCl = MnCl2 +H2O + Cl2

$Mn4+ + 2e = Mn2+ \quad | \; 2 \; 1$

$2Cl- - 2e = Cl2 \mid 2\ I$

Since two ions of Cl- are required to get 2 electrons and 2 Cl- are necessary to produce MnCl2. We have to put 4 in front of HCl.

$MnO2 + 4HCl = MnCl2 + H2O + Cl2$

Now balance H and O:

$MnO2 + 4HCl = MnCl2 + 2H2O + Cl2$

28. Cl2 + KOH = KCl + KClO3 + H2O

$Cl2 + 2e = 2Cl- \mid 2\ I\ 5$
$Cl2 - 10e = 2Cl5+ \mid 10\ 5\ I$

It is a hard one!
Put 5 in front of KCl according to electronic balance.

$Cl2 + KOH = 5KCl + KClO3 + H2O$
Now we have I K on the left and 6 K on the right. Put 6 in front of KOH.

$Cl2 + 6KOH = 5KCl + KClO3 + H2O$

Now balance Cl.

$3Cl2 + 6KOH = 5KCl + KClO3 + H2O$

And balance H and O

$3Cl2 + 6KOH = 5KCl + KClO3 + 3H2O$

29. KMnO4 + NH3 = MnO2 + KOH + N2 + H2O

Mn7+ + 3e = Mn4+ |3 I 2

2N3- - 6e = 2N |6 2 I

2KMnO4 + 2NH3 = 2MnO2 + 2KOH + N2 + 2H2O

30. Mg + HNO3 = Mg(NO3)2 + NH4NO3 + H2O

Mg - 2e = Mg2+ |2 I 4
N5+ + 8e = N3- | 8 4 I

4Mg + HNO3 = 4Mg(NO3)2 + NH4NO3 + H2O

Balance NO3

4Mg + 10HNO3 = 4Mg(NO3)2 + NH4NO3 + H2O

Balance H and O

4Mg + 10HNO3 = 4Mg(NO3)2 + NH4NO3 + 3H2O

Stoichiometry

Problems with answers and solutions

1. How much Copper is produced if 200 ml of IM CuSO4 solution reacts with I g of iron powder?
CuSO4 + Fe = FeSO4 + Cu.

2. How many liters of CO2 are produced if I liter of C2H6 is burnt completely?
2C2H6 + 7O2 = 4CO2 + 6H2O

3. How many grams of iron are produced when I kg of Fe2O3 is completely reduced by hydrogen? How many liters of hydrogen are required?

$Fe2O3 + 3H2 = 2Fe + 3H2O$

4. How much NaCl is produced if 100g of Na reacts with 10 liters of Cl2?
Which initial reactant will be left over?

$2Na + Cl2 = 2NaCl$

5. How many grams of Na2SO4 are produced if 1 Liter of 1M NaOH reacts with 1 Liter of 0.5 M H2SO4? Which initial reactant will be left over?

$2NaOH + H2SO4 = Na2SO4 + 2H2O.$

6. How many grams of K2SO4 are produced if 0.5 liters of 0.1M solution of KOH reacts with 0.3 liters of 0.2 M solution of H2SO4? Which initial reactant will be left over?

$H2SO4 + 2KOH = K2SO4 + 2H2O$

7. How many grams of Ba(NO3)2 are produced if 0.3 liters of 0.1 M solution of HNO3 reacts with 0.1 liters of 0.3 M solution of Ba(OH)2? Which initial reactant will be left over?

$2HNO3 + Ba (OH)2 = Ba(NO3)2 + 2H2O.$

8. How many liters of 0.2M solutions of NaOH are required to produce 0.7 liters of 0.5M solution of Na3PO4 in the following reaction?

$H3PO4 + 3NaOH = Na3PO4 + 3H2O$
How many moles of H3PO4 will be spent?

9. How many liters of H2 will be produced if 10 grams of Mg reacts with 0.5 liters of 0.1M solution of H2SO4? Which initial reactant will be left over?

$Mg + H2SO4 = MgSO4 + H2$

10. How many grams of Al are required to produce 3 liters of H2 if Al reacts with 0.1M solutions of HCl? How many liters of solution of HCl will be spent?

$2Al + 6HCl = 2AlCl3 + 3H2$

11. How many grams of AgCl will be produced if 0.5 liters of 0.3M solution of AgNO3 reacts with 1 liter of 0.5M solution of CaCL2? Which initial reactant will be left over?

$2AgNO3 + CaCl2 = 2AgCl + Ca(NO3)2$

12. How many liters of 0.1 M solution of H2SO4 are required to produce 33 g of ZnSO4 and how many grams of Zn(OH)2 are spent?

$Zn(OH)2 + H2SO4 = ZnSO4 + 2H2O$

13. How many liters of 0.3 M solution of H2SO4 are required to produce 9 g of Al2(SO4)3 and how many grams of Al(OH)3 are spent?

$2Al(OH)3 + 3H2SO4 = Al2(SO4)3 + 6H2O$

14. How many liters of NH3 are required to produce 2 liters of 0.1M solution of NH4HCO3
How many liters of CO2 will be spent in the following reaction?

$NH3 + CO2 + H2O = NH4HCO3$

15. How many liters of CO2 are produced if 200 grams of CaCO3 react with SiO2 in the following reaction?

$CaCO3 + SiO2 = CaSiO3 + CO2$

16. How many liters of O2 are required to oxidize 60 grams of FeS2 to Fe2O3?

$4FeS2 + 11O2 = 2Fe2O3 + 8SO2$

17. How many liters of oxygen gas will be required to burn 3 moles of methane completely?

$CH4 + 2O2 = CO2 + 2H2O$

18. Calculate the number of liters of Oxygen required to completely react with 51g of ammonia.

$4NH3 + 5O2 = 4NO + 6H2O$

19. Calculate the mass of silver nitrate in grams required to completely react with 7 moles of lead?

$Pb + 2AgNO3 -> Pb(NO3)2 + 2Ag$

20. Calculate the mass of carbon in grams that must react with Oxygen to produce $12x10^{23}$ molecules of Carbon Dioxide (CO2)

$C + O2 = CO2$

21. How many liters of hydrogen gas are required to completely hydrogenate 952 g of 2-butene?

$CH3-CH=CH-CH3 + H2 = CH3-CH2-CH2-CH3$

22. How many grams of barium chloride is required to completely precipitate barium sulfate from 1 liter of 0.3M H2SO4?

$H_2SO_4 + BaCl_2 -= BaSO_4 + 2HCl$

23. What mass of potassium hydroxide is required to react completely with 1 liter of 0.1M sulfuric acid solution to produce potassium sulfate? How many grams of K_2SO_4 will be produced?

$2KOH + H_2SO_4 \rightarrow 2H_2O + K_2SO_4$

24. What volume of 0.2M NaOH is required to completely neutralize 50.0 mL of 0.3M HCl?

$NAOH + HCl = NACl + H_2O$

25. How many grams of $MgCl_2$ are produced if 0.5 liters of 0.5 M solution of HCL react with $Mg(OH)_2$. How much $Mg(OH)_2$ is spent?

$Mg(OH)_2 + 2HCl = MgCl_2 + 2H_2O$

26. How many grams of $KClO_3$ would be required to produce 3 liters of O_2? How many grams of KCl are produced?

$2KClO_3 = 3O_2 + 2KCl$

27. How many liters of 0.5M solution of HCl is required to completely react with 25.0 g of Aluminum? How many liters of H_2 are produced?

$2Al + 6 HCl = 2AlCl_3 + 3H_2$

28. How many grams of Nitrogen would be required to completely react with 11.2 liters of hydrogen to give ammonia? How many grams of ammonia are produced?

$N_2 + 3 H_2 = 2 NH_3$

29. Calculate the 0.5 M sulfuric acid volume in milliliters required to completely neutralize 100 ml of 1 M solution of KOH?

$H2SO4 + 2KOH = K2SO4 + 2H2O$

What is the K+ ion concentration at the end of the reaction?

30. How many grams of Fe2O3 are required to completely react with 3 moles of Al?
$2Al + Fe2O3 = 2Fe + Al2O3$

31. How much Copper is produced if 200 ml of IM CuSO4 solution reacts with 26 g of iron powder?
$CuSO4 + Fe = FeSO4 + Cu.$

32. How much KCl is produced if 70g of K reacts with 10 liters of Cl2? Which initial reactant will be left over? $2K + Cl2 = 2KCl$

33. How many grams of K2SO4 are produced if I liter of IM KOH reacts with I Liter of 0.5 M H2SO4? Which initial reactant will be left over?
$2KOH + H2SO4 = K2SO4 + 2H2O.$

34. How many grams of K2SO4 is produced if 0.I liter of 0.IM solution of KOH reacts with 0.I Liter of 0.I M solution of H2SO4? Which initial reactant will be left over?
$H2SO4 + 2KOH = K2SO4 + 2H2O$

35. How many grams of Ba(NO3)2 are produced if 0.I liter of 0.I M solution of HNO3 reacts with 0.I liter of 0.I M solution of Ba(OH)2? Which initial reactant will be left over?
$2HNO3 + Ba (OH)2 = Ba(NO3)2 + 2H2O.$

36. How many liters of 0.IM solutions of NaOH are required to produce I liters of 0.IM solution of Na3PO4 in the following reaction:
$H3PO4 + 3NaOH = Na3PO4 + 3H2O$

41

37. How many liters of H2 will be produced if 10 grams of Ca reacts with 1 liter of 0.1M solution of H2SO4? Which initial reactant will be left over?

Ca + H2SO4 = CaSO4 + H2

38. How many grams of AgCl will be produced if 0.1 liter of 0.1M solution of AgNO3 reacts with 1 liter of 0.1M solution of CaCL2? Which initial reactant will be left over?

2AgNO3 + CaCl2 = 2AgCl + Ca(NO3)2

39. How many liters of 0.1 M solution of H2SO4 are required to produce 5 g of ZnSO4? How many grams of Zn(OH)2 are spent?

Zn(OH)2 + H2SO4 = ZnSO4 + 2H2O

40. How many grams of ZnSO4 are produced if 7 g of Zn(OH)2 react with 03L of 0.1M solution of H2SO4?

Zn(OH)2 + H2SO4 = ZnSO4 + 2H2O

41. What mass of Sodium hydroxide is required to react completely with 0.5 liters of 0.5M sulfuric acid solution to produce Sodium sulfate?

42. What volume of 0.1M Ca(OH)2 solution is required to completely neutralize 5.0 mL of 0.3M HCl solution?

Ca(OH)2 + 2HCl = CaCl2 + 2H2O

43. How many grams of MgCl2 are produced if 0.1 L of 0.1 M solution of HCL reacts with Mg(OH)2. How much Mg(OH)2 is spent?

Mg(OH)2 + 2HCl = MgCl2 + 2H2O

44. How many grams of KClO3 would be required to produce 22.4 liters of O2? How many grams of KCl are produced?
2KClO3 = 3O2 + 2KCl

45. How many liters of 0.1M solution of HCl is required to completely react with 5.0 g of Aluminum? How many liters of H2 are produced?
2Al + 6 HCl =2AlCl3 + 3H2

46. How many liters of Nitrogen would be required to completely react with 5.6 liters of hydrogen to produce ammonia? How many grams of ammonia are produced?
N2 + 3 H2 = 2 NH3

47. Calculate the volume of 0.1 M sulfuric acid solution in milliliters required to completely neutralize 100 ml of 0.1 M solution of KOH?
H2SO4 + 2KOH = K2SO4 + 2H2O

48. How many liters of NH3 are required to produce 10 grams of NH4HCO3?
How many liters of CO2 will be spent in the following reaction?
NH3 + CO2 + H2O = NH4HCO3

49. How many liters of 0.1 M solution of H2SO4 are required to produce 5 g of Al2(SO4)3 and how many grams of Al(OH)3 are spent?
2Al(OH)3 + 3H2SO4 = Al2(SO4)3 + 6H2O

50. How many grams of Al is required to produce 11.2 liters of H2 if Al reacts with 0.1M solutions of HCl? How many liters of solution of HCl will be spent?
2Al + 6HCl = 2AlCl3 + 3H2

Answers and Solutions

1. How much Copper is produced if 200 ml of 1M CuSO4 solution reacts with 1 g of iron powder?

CuSO4 + Fe = FeSO4 + Cu.

Solution: The mass of one mole of CuSO4 is $64 + 32 + 16*4 = 160g$. How did we get it?

The mass of Cu is 64, the mass of S is 32, and the mass of O is 16. $(16*4=64)$

An IM solution of CuSO4 has one mole per liter. It means one liter of CuSO4 contains 98 g of H2SO4.

We have 200 ml of CuSO4. How many grams of CuSO4 in 200 ml? 1000ml is 160g of CuSO4.

200 ml is X g of CuSO4.

$X = 200ml * 160g/ 1000ml = 32$ g of CuSO4.

The mass of Cu is 64. One mole of Cu is 64 g.

This equation shows that one mole of CuSO4 produces one mole of Cu. 160 g of CuSO4 produce 64 g of Cu.

32 g of CuSO4 produce X gram of Cu

$X = 32g * 64g / 160g = 12.8$ g Cu

If we have enough Fe, 32 g CuSO4 can produce 12.8 g Cu.

Do we have enough Fe to react completely with 32 g of H2SO4?

The mass of Fe is 56. One mole of Fe is 56g.

The equation shows that one mole of H2SO4 requires one mole of Fe. 160 g of CuSO4 requires 56 g of Fe,

We have 32 g of CuSO4. How many grams of Fe do we need for a complete reaction?

160 g CuSO4 - 56g of Fe.

32g CuSO4 - Xg of Fe.

$X = 32 * 56 / 160 = 11.2$ g of Fe is required.

We have only 1 g of Fe. Not all H2SO4 will react with 1 g of Fe, and we cannot get 12.8 g of Cu. Before calculating how much Cu is produced, we must determine which reactant is limited and which is in excess. How can we do that? We should start our solution with the proportion:

32 g of $CuSO_4$ required 11.2 g of Fe
X g of $CuSO_4$ required 1 g of Fe
X = 32 * 1 /11.2 = 2.86 g $CuSO_4$
Only 2.86 g of $CuSO_4$ will participate in a reaction with 11.2g of Fe. We have an excess of $CuSO_4$, and Fe is a limited reactant.
We should use a limited reactant to calculate how much Cu is produced.
One mole of Fe produces one mole of Cu.
56 g of Fe produces 64 g of Cu.
1 g of Fe produces X g of Cu
X = 1 * 64 / 56 = 1.14g of Cu.

Answer: 1.14g of Cu is produced.

2. How many liters of CO2 are produced if 1 liter of C2H6 is burnt completely?

2C2H6 + 7O2 = 4CO2 + 6H2O

Solution: The chemical equation shows that 2 moles of C2H6 produce 4 moles of CO2.

In normal conditions, the volume of one mole of gas is 22.4 liters.
Two moles of C2H6 equal 22.4 * 2 = 44.8 liters.
4 moles of CO2 equal 22.4 * 4 = 89.6 liters
44.8 liters of C2H6 produce 89.6 liters of CO2.
1 liter of C2H6 produces X liters of CO2.
X = 1 * 89.6 / 44.8 = 2 liters of CO2

Answer: 2 liters of CO2 is produced.

3. How many grams of iron are produced when 1 kg of Fe2O3 is entirely reduced by hydrogen?

How many liters of hydrogen are required?

Fe2O3 + 3H2 = 2Fe + 3H2O

From the equation, we can see that one mole of Fe2O3 produces 2 moles of Fe.

One mole of Fe2O3 is 56*2 + 16*3=160g.

One mole of Fe is 56g. Two moles of Fe are 56*2=112g.

160g of Fe2O3 produce 112g of Fe 1 kg = 1000 g.

1000g of Fe2O3 produces Xg of Fe.

X= 1000 * 112/ 160 = 700g of Fe is produced.

How many liters of H2 are required?

From the equation, we see that one mole of Fe2O3 requires 3 moles of H2.

One mole of Fe2O3 is 56*2 + 16*3=160g.

3 moles of H2 equal 6 g.

160 g of Fe2O3 consume 6 g of H2

700 g of Fe2O3 consume X g of H2 X = 700 g * 6 g / 160 g =26.3 g

1 mole of H2 is 2 g and occupies 22.4 L (1 mole of any gas occupies 22.4 L)

26.3 g of H2 occupies X L

X = 26.3 g * 22.4 L / 2 g = 294 L of H2

Answer: 700g Fe is produced, and 294 L of H2 is required.

4. How much NaCl is produced if 100g of Na reacts with 10 liters of Cl2?

Which initial reactant will be left over? 2Na + Cl2 = 2NaCl

First, we must determine which reactant is limited and which will be left over.

The equation shows that 2 moles of Na react with one mole of Cl2.

2 moles of Na is 23*2=46g. One mole of Cl2 is 35*2=70g.

46 g of Na reacts with 70g of Cl2.

How many g of Cl2 do we have?

One mole of gas is 22.4L. It means:

70g of Cl2 is 22.4 L.

X g of Cl2 is 10 L.

X = 70 * 10 / 22.4 = 31.25g. 10 L of Cl2 is 31.25g.

2 moles of Na react with one mole of Cl2.

46 g of Na reacts with 70 g of Cl2. We have 100 g of Na. How much

Cl2 is required in grams?

100 g of Na reacts with X g of Cl2.

X = 100 g * 70 g /46 g = 152 g of Cl2.

We need 152 g of Cl2 per reaction, but we have only 31.25g. It means Cl2 is limited, and Na will be left over. We have to use the limited reactant, Cl2, to calculate how much NaCl is produced.

The equation shows that one mole of Cl2 produces 2 moles of NaCl.

One mole of Cl2 is 35*2=70 g and two moles of NaCl is

(23 + 35) * 2=116g.

One mole of Cl2 produces 2 moles of NaCl.

70g of Cl2 produces 116g of NaCl.

31.25g of Cl2 produces X g of NaCl.

X = 31.25 * 116 / 70 =51.79 g of NaCl.

Answer: 51.79 g of NaCl is produced. Na will be left over.

5. How many grams of Na2SO4 are produced if 1 liter of 1M NaOH reacts with 1 Liter of 0.5 M H2SO4? Which initial reactant will be left over?

2NaOH + H2SO4 = Na2SO4 + 2H2O.

First, let us calculate how many grams of NaOH and H2SO4 we have. Then determine which reactant is limited.

The mass of one mole of NaOH is 23 + 16 + 1=40g.

1 liter of 1M of NaOH contains 40g of NaOH.

The mass of one mole of H2SO4 is 2 + 32 + 16*4 = 98g.

1 liter of 1M solution of H2SO4 contains 98g H2SO4.

We have a 0.5M solution of H2SO4.

1 L of 1 M of H2SO4 contains 98g.

1 L of 0.5M of H2SO4 contains X g.

X=0.5 * 98 / 1 = 49g. H2SO4.

From the equation, we see that two moles of NaOH react with one mole of H2SO4.

One mole of NaOH is 40g, 2 moles are 80g.

80g NaOH reacts with 98g of H2SO4.

40g NaOH reacts with X g of H2SO4.

X = 40g * 98g /80g = 49g H2SO4.

We found that for an existing amount of NaOH (40g), we need 49 g of H2SO4.

Since 1 L of 0.5M solution of H2SO4 contains 49g H2SO4, we have enough H2SO4 for a complete reaction with the existing amount of NaOH. No reactant is left over. We can use either one to calculate how much Na2SO4 will be produced. Let us use NaOH.

The mass of one mole of Na2SO4 is 23*2 + 32 + 16*4=46 + 32 + 64= 142g.

From the equation, we see that 2 mole of NaOH produces one mole of Na2SO4.

80g NaOH produces 142g of Na2SO4.

40g NaOH produce X g Na2SO4.

X = 40 * 142 /80 = 71g.

Answer: 71 g of Na2SO4 is produced.

6. How many grams of K2SO4 is produced if 0.5 liter of 0.1M solution of KOH reacts with 0.3 Liter of 0.2 M solution of H2SO4? Which initial reactant will be left over?

H2SO4 + 2KOH = K2SO4 + 2H2O

Let us calculate how much KOH and H2SO4 we have in grams.

Mass of one mole of KOH is 39 + 16 + 1 = 56g

1 L of 1M solution of KOH contains 56g of KOH.

1 L of 1 M of KOH - 56 g

1 L of 0.1M of KOH - X g X = 56 g * 0.1 M/1 M = 5.6g of KOH

Then 1 L of 0.1 M solution will contain 5.6 g KOH.

We have 0.5 L of KOH solution.

1 L of KOH - 5.6 g

0.5 L of KOH - X g

X = 0.5L * 5.6g / 1 L= 2.8 g KOH. So, we have 2.8 g KOH.

The mass of H_2SO_4 is $2 + 32 + 16*4 = 98$ g.

1 L of 1 M of H_2SO_4 solution contains 98 g.

1 L of 0.2 M of H_2SO_4 solution contains X g.

$X = 0.2 * 98 / 1 = 19.6$ g of H_2SO_4.

1 L of 0.2 M solution contains 19.6 g H_2SO_4.

0.3 L of 0.2 M solution contains X g.

$X = 0.3 * 19.6 / 1 = 5.8$ g. We have 5.8 g of H_2SO_4.

We have 2.8 g of KOH and 5.8 g of H_2SO_4. Which reactant is limited?

From our equation, 2 mole of KOH reacts with one mole of H_2SO_4.

$56 * 2 = 112$ g KOH reacts with 98 g of H_2SO_4.

2.8 g of KOH reacts with X g of H_2SO_4.

$X = 2.8g * 98 g / 112 g = 2.45$ g H_2SO_4.

For 2.8 g KOH, we need 2.45 g H_2SO_4, and we have 5.8 g H_2SO_4.

It means that H_2SO_4 will be left over.

KOH is a limited reactant, and we have to use KOH to calculate how much K_2SO_4 is produced.

The mass of one mole of K_2SO_4 is $39*2 + 32 + 64 = 174$ g.

Two moles of KOH produce one mole of K_2SO_4.

112 g KOH produces 174g K_2SO_4.

2.8 g KOH produce X g K_2SO_4.

$X = 2.8 g * 174 g / 112 g = 4.35$ g K_2SO_4.

Answer: KOH is a limited reactant. 4.35 g of K2SO4 is produced.

7. How many grams of Ba(NO3)2 are produced if 0.3 liter of 0.1 M solution of HNO3 reacts with 0.1 liter of 0.3 M solution of Ba(OH)2? Which initial reactant will be left over?

2HNO3 + Ba (OH)2 = Ba(NO3)2 + 2H2O.

Let us calculate how much HNO_3 and Ba $(OH)_2$ we have in grams.

The mass of one mole of HNO_3 is $1 + 14 + 16*3 = 63$ g

1 L of 1M solution of HNO_3 contains 63 g.

0.3 L of 1 M solution of HNO_3 contains X g.

X = 0.3 * 63 /1 = 18.9 g of HNO_3.

0.3 L of 1 M solution of HNO_3 contains 18.9 g.

0.3 L of 0.1 M solution of HNO_3 contains X g.

X = 0.1 M * 18.9 g /1 M= 1.89 g.

So, we have 1.89 g of HNO_3.

The mass of one mole of $Ba(OH)_2$ = 137 + 2 * (16 + 1) = 171 g.

1 L of 1 M solution of $Ba(OH)_2$ contains 171 g.

1 L of 0.3 M solution of $Ba(OH)_2$ contains X g.

X = 0.3 M * 171 g /1 M = 51.3 g.

1 L of 0.3 M solution of $Ba(OH)_2$ contains 51.3 g.

0.1 L of 0.3 M solution of $Ba(OH)_2$ contains X g.

X = 0.1 L * 51.3 g/ 1 L = 5.13 g.

So, we have 5.13 g of $Ba(OH)_2$ and 1.89 g of HNO_3. Which reactant is limited, and which will be left over?

The equation shows that 2 moles of HNO_3 react with one mole of $Ba(OH)_2$.

One mole of HNO_3 is 63 g. Two moles are 63 * 2 = 126 g.

One mole of $Ba(OH)_2$ is 171 g.

126 g of HNO_3 react with 171 g of $Ba(OH)_2$.

1.89 g of HNO_3 react with X g of $Ba(OH)_2$.

X = 1.89g * 171g / 126g = 2.57 g $Ba(OH)_2$.

This reactant will be left over since we have 5.13 g of $Ba(OH)_2$ and need only 2.57g.

We should use HNO_3 to calculate how much $Ba(NO_3)_2$ is produced.

The mass of one mole of $Ba(NO_3)_2$ is 137 + 2(14 + 15*3) = 137 + 2 (14 + 48) = 261 g.

Two moles of HNO_3 produce one mole of $Ba(NO_3)_2$.

126 g of HNO_3 produces 261 g $Ba(NO_3)_2$.

1.89 g of HNO_3 produce X g of $Ba(NO_3)_2$.

X = 1.89 * 261 /126 = 3.92 g of $Ba(NO_3)_2$.

Answer: 3.92 g of Ba(NO3)2 is produced. HNO3 is a limited reactant. Ba (OH)2 will be left over.

8. How many liters of 0.2M solutions of NaOH are required to produce 0.7 liters of 0.5M solution of Na3PO4 in the following reaction:

H3PO4 + 3NaOH = Na3PO4 + 3H2O

How many moles of H3PO4 will be spent?

First, calculate how many grams in 0.7 L of 0.5M solution of Na3PO4.

The mass of one mole of Na3PO4 is 23 * 3 + 31 + 16*4 = 164 g.

1 L of 1M solution of Na3PO4 contains 164 g of Na3PO4.

1 L of 0.5 M solution of Na3PO4 contains X g of Na3PO4.

X = 0.5 M * 164g / 1 M = 82 g of Na3PO4.

1 L of 0.5 M solution of Na3PO4 contains 82 g.

0.7 L of 0.5 M solution of Na3PO4 contains X g.

X = 0.7 L * 82 g /1 L = 57.4 g of Na3PO4.

So, 57.4 g of Na3PO4 is produced.

How many grams of NaOH do we need for that?

From the equation, 3 moles of NaOH are required to produce one mole of Na3PO4.

The mass of one mole of NaOH is 23 + 16 + 1 = 40 g. 3 moles are 40 * 3 = 120g.

120 grams of NaOH produce 164 g of Na3PO4.

X g of NaOH produces 57.4 g of Na3PO4.

X= 120 g * 57.4 g /164 g = 42 g.

We need 42 g of NaOH to produce 57.4 g of Na3PO4.

Let us calculate how many grams of NaOH are in 1 L of 0.2 M solution of NaOH.

1 L of 1 M solution of NaOH contains 40 g of NaOH.

1 L 0.2 M solution of NaOH contains X g of NaOH.

X = 0.2 M * 40g / 1 L = 8g

Now we can calculate how many liters of 0.2 M solution of NaOH we need.

1 L contains 8 g NaOH.

X L contains 42 g NaOH.

X = 1 * 42 / 8 = 5.25 L.

Answer: 5.25 L of 0.2M solutions of NaOH are required to produce 0.7 liters of 0.5M solution of Na3PO4

9. How many liters of H2 will be produced if 10 grams of Mg reacts with 0.5 liters of 0.1M solution of H2SO4? Which initial reactant will be left over?

Mg + H2SO4 = MgSO4 + H2

Let us calculate how much H2SO4 we have in grams.

The mass of one mole of H2SO4 is 2 + 32 + 64 = 98 g. H2SO4

I L of IM solution contains 98 g H2SO4. We have only 0.5 L

0.5 L of IM solution contains X.

X =0.5L * 98 g / I L = 49 g. H2SO4

I M solution contains 49 g H2SO4.

0.I M solution contains X g H2SO4.

X = 0.I M * 49g/I M = 4.9 g H2SO4

So, 0.5 L of a 0.I M solution contains 4.9 g of H2SO4.

Let us calculate how much H2SO4 we need to completely react with I0 g of Mg.

From the equation, one mole of Mg reacts with one mole of H2SO4.

The mass of one mole of Mg is 24 g.

24 g of Mg reacts with 98 g of H2SO4.

I0 g of Mg reacts with X g of H2SO4.

X = I0g * 98g / 24g =40.8 g

We have 4.9 g of H2SO4, but we need 40.8 g. It means that H2SO4 is limited, and Mg will be left over.

To calculate how many liters of H2 are produced, we have to use H2SO4.

From the equation, one mole of H2SO4 produces one mole of H2, and one mole of H2 is 22.4 L

98 g of H2SO4 produce 22.4 L H2.

4.9 g of H2SO4 produce X L of H2.

X=4.9 * 22.4 / 98 = I.I2 L H2.

Answer: 1.12 L H2 is produced. Mg is left over.

10. How many grams of Al are required to produce 3 liters of H2 if Al reacts with 0.1M solutions of HCl? How many liters of solution of HCl will be spent?

2Al + 6HCl = 2AlCl3 + 3H2

Let us calculate how much Al is required to produce 3 L of H2.

The equation shows that 2 moles of Al produce 3 moles of H2.

2 moles of Al equals 27 * 2 = 54 g. 3 moles of H2 is equal to 3*22.4 L = 67.2 L.

56 g of Al produces 67.2 L of H2.

X g of Al produces 3 L H2.

X = 56 g * 3L /67.2 L = 2.5 g Al.

Now let us calculate how much HCl is required to produce 3 L of H2.

From the equation, 6 moles of HCL produce 3 moles of H2.

The mass of one mole of HCl is 1 + 35 = 36g. The mass of 6 moles is 36 g * 6 = 216 g.

As we calculated before, 3 moles of H2 occupy 67.2 L.

216 g of HCl produces 67.2 L H2.

X g of HCl produces 3 L of H2.

X = 216 g * 3 L/67.2 L = 9.6 g of HCl.

If 1 L of 1M solution of HCL is 36 g/L, then 1 L of 0.1 M solution is 3.6 g/L.

3.6 g of HCl is in 1 L of 0.1 M solution.

9.6 g of HCl is in X L of 0.1 M solution.

X = 9.6 g * 1L/ 3.6 g = 2.67 L.

Answer: 2.5 g Al and 2.67 L of 0.1 M solution of HCl are required to produce 3 L of H2

11. How many grams of AgCl will be produced if 0.5 liters of 0.3M solution of AgNO3 reacts with 1 liter of 0.5M solution of CaCL2? Which initial reactant will be left over?

2AgNO3 + CaCl2 = 2AgCl + Ca(NO3)2

Let us calculate how much of each reactant we have in grams. Let us start with AgNO3.

The mass of one mole of AgNO3 is $108 + 14 + 48 = 170$ g.

I L of IM solution of AgNO3 contains 170g of AgNO3.

0.5 L of IM solution contains X g of AgNO3.

X = 0.5L * 170g /1L=85 g of AgNO3.

0.5L of I M solution of AgNO3 contains 85g of AgNO3.

0.3 M solution of AgNO3 contains X g of ArNO3.

X = 0.3 * 85 / 1 = 25.5g of ArNO3.

0.5 L of 0.3 M solution of AgNO3 contains 25.5 g AgNO3.

Let us calculate how much CaCl2 we have in grams.

The mass of one mole of CaCl2 is $40 + 35*2=110$g.

I L of IM solution of CaCl2 contains 110g of CaCl2.

I L of 0.5M solution contains X g of CaCl2.

X = 0.5M * 110g/1M = 55g of CaCl2.

I L of 0.5 M solution of CaCl2 contains 55g of CaCl2.

From the equation, 2 moles of AgNO3 react with one mole of CaCl2.

340g (170 *2) AgNO3 react with 110 g of CaCl2.

25.5 g AgNO3 reacts with X g CaCl2.

X = 25.5 * 110 /340 = 8.25 g CaCl2.

Since 25.5 g of AgNO3 and 8.25 g of CaCl2 are required to complete the reaction, and we have 55g of CaCl2, CaCl2 will be left over. AgNO3 is a limited reactant, and we should use AgNO3 to calculate how much AgCl is produced.

The mass of one mole of AgCl is $108 + 35=143$ g.

From the equation, 2 moles of AgNO3 produce 2 moles of AgCl.

Two moles of AgNO3 equal 340g, and 2 moles of AgCl are equivalent to 286g.

340 g of AgNO3 produce 286 g AgCl.

25.5g of AgNO3 produce X g AgCl.

X = 25.5 * 286 /340 = 21.45 g of AgCl.

Answer: 21.45 g AgCl are produced. CaCl2 will be left over.

12. How many liters of 0.1 M solution of H2SO4 are

required to produce 33 g of ZnSO4? How many grams of Zn(OH)2 are spent?

Zn(OH)2 + H2SO4 = ZnSO4 + 2H2O

Let us calculate how much H2SO4 we have in 1 L of 0.1 M solution in grams.

The mass of H2SO4 is $2 + 32 + 64 = 98$ g.

1 L of 1 M solution contains 98g of H2SO4.

1 L of 0.1 M solution contains X g of H2SO4.

X = 0.1 M * 98g / 1M = 9.8g of H2SO4.

The mass of one mole of ZnSO4 is $65 + 32 + 64 = 161$ g

From the equation, one mole of H2SO4 produces one mole of ZnSO4.

98 g H2SO4 produce 161 g ZnSO4.

X g H2SO4 produces 33 g ZnSO4.

X = 98g * 33g / 161g = 20 g of H2SO4.

1 L of 0.1 M solution contains 9.8 g H2SO4.

X L of 0.1 M solution contains 20g H2SO4.

X = 1 L * 20 g / 9.8 g = 2 L H2SO4.

How many grams of Zn(OH)2 are spent?

The mass of one mole of Zn(OH)2 is $108 + (16 + 1)*2 = 142$ g.

From the equation, one mole of Zn(OH)2 produces one mole of ZnSO4.

142 g of Zn(OH)2 produce 161 g of ZnSO4.

X g of Zn(OH)2 produce 33 g of ZnSO4.

X = 142g * 33g / 161g = 29.1 g of Zn(OH)2.

Answer: 2 L of 0.1 M solution of H2SO4 and 29.1 g of Zn(OH)2 are required to produce 33 g of ZnSO4.

13. How many liters of 0.3 M solution of H2SO4 are required to produce 9 g of Al2(SO4)3 and how many grams of Al(OH)3 are spent?

2Al(OH)3 + 3H2SO4 = Al2(SO4)3 + 6H2O

Let us calculate how much H2SO4 we have in grams in 1 L of 0.3 M solution.

The mass of H2SO4 is $2 + 32 + 64 = 98$ g.

1 L of 1 M solution contains 98g of H_2SO_4.

1 L of 0.3 M solution contains X g of H_2SO_4.

X = 0.3 M * 98g / 1M = 29.4g.

The mass of one mole $Al_2(SO_4)_3$ is 27*2 + (32 + 64) * 3 = 342 g.

From the equation, 3 moles of H_2SO_4 are required to produce one mole of $Al_2(SO_4)_3$.

294g (98 * 3) H_2SO_4 produce 342 g $Al_2(SO_4)_3$.

X g H_2SO_4 produce 9 g $Al_2(SO_4)_3$.

X = 9g * 294g /342g=7.74 g of H_2SO_4.

1 L of 0.3M solution of H_2SO_4 contains 29.4 g of H_2SO_4.

X L of 0.3 M solution of H_2SO_4 contains 7.74 g of H_2SO_4.

X = 1L * 7.74 g/29.4 g = 0.26 L of 0.3 M solution of H_2SO_4.

How many grams of $Al(OH)_3$ is spent?

The mass of one mole of $Al(OH)_3$ is 27 + 17*3 = 78 g.

From the equation, 2 moles of $Al(OH)_3$ are required to produce one $Al_2(SO_4)_3$ mole.

156 g (2*78) of $Al(OH)_3$ produce 342 g of $Al_2(SO_4)_3$.

X g of $Al(OH)_3$ produce 9 g of $Al_2(SO_4)_3$.

X = 156 g * 9 g / 342 g = 4.1 g of $Al(OH)_3$

Answer: To produce 9 g of Al2(SO4)3, 0.26 L of 0.3M solution of H2SO4 and 4.1 g of Al(OH)3 are required.

14. How many liters of NH3 are required to produce 2 liters of 0.1M solution of NH4HCO3?

How many liters of CO2 will be spent in the following reaction?

NH3 + CO2 + H2O = NH4HCO3

When you need to find an answer in liters, it is not always necessary to calculate how many grams of reactant are spent or produced. Sometimes, it is enough to calculate how many moles are involved.

In this problem, we calculate moles, and knowing that one mole of gas occupies 22.4 L, we can calculate liters.

1 L of 0.1M solution of NH_4HCO_3 contains 0.1 moles of NH_4HCO_3.

2 L of 0.1 M solutions of NH4HCO3 contain X moles of NH4HCO3.

X = 2L * 0.1 moles/1L = 0.2 moles.

From the equation, one mole of NH3 produces one mole of NH4HCO3.

1 mole NH3 produces 1 mole NH4HCO3.

X mole of NH3 produces 0.2 moles of NH4HCO3.

X = 1 mole * 0.2 moles/1 mole = 0.2 mole.

1 mole of NH3 occupies 22.4 L.

0.2 mole of NH3 occupies X L.

X = 0.2 mole * 22.4 L /1 mole = 4.48 L.

How many liters of CO2 are spent? The solution is the same as for NH3.

From the equation, one mole of CO2 produces one mole of NH4HCO3.

X moles of CO2 produce 0.2 moles of NH4HCO3.

X = 0.2 moles, and the volume is 4.48 L.

Answer: 4.48 L of NH3 and 4.48 L of CO2 are required to produce 2 liters of a 0.1M solution of NH4HCO3

15. How many liters of CO2 are produced if 200 grams of CaCO3 reacts with SiO2 in the following reaction?

CaCO3 + SiO2 = CaSiO3 + CO2

Again, we don't have to calculate grams. From the equation, one mole of CaCO3 produces one mole of CO2.

Let us calculate how many moles of CaCO3 there are in 100 g of CaCO3.

The mass of one mole of CaCO3 is 40 + 12 + 48=100 g.

We have 200 g CaCO3, which means we have two moles of CaCO3.

Two moles of CaCO3 produce two moles of CO2, and 2 moles of CO2 is 22.4 L * 2 = 44.8 L.

Answer: 44.8 L of CO2 is produced from 200 g of CaCO3.

16. How many liters of O2 are required to oxidize 60 grams of FeS2 to Fe2O3?

4FeS2 + 11O2 = 2Fe2O3 + 8SO2

Let us calculate how many moles of FeS2 we have in 100 g.

The mass of one mole of FeS2 is 56 + 32*2 =120 g.

We have 60 g of FeS2, and it is 0.5 mole.

I mole – 120 g

X mole – 60 g

X = 1*60/120 = 0.5 moles

From the equation, 4 moles of FeS2 require 11 moles of O2.

0.5 mole of FeS2 required X mole of O2.

X = 0.5 moles * 11 moles /4 moles = 1.38 moles of O2.

I mole of O2 occupies 22.4 L.

1.38 mole occupies X L.

X = 1.38 mole * 22.4 L /1 mole = 30.9 L O2.

Answer: 30.9 L O2 is required to oxidize 60 grams of FeS2 to Fe2O3.

17. How many liters of oxygen gas will be required to burn 3 moles of methane completely?

CH4 + 2O2 = CO2 + 2H2O

From the equation, one mole of CH4 requires 2 moles of O2.

3 moles of CH4 require X moles of O2.

X = 3 moles * 2 moles/1 mole = 6 moles of O2.

One mole of O2 occupies 22.4 L.

Six moles of O2 occupy X L.

X = 6 moles * 22.4 L / 1 mole =134 L O2.

Answer: 134 L of O2 are required to completely burn 3 moles of CH3.

18. Calculate the number of liters of Oxygen required to completely react with 51g of ammonia.

4NH3 + 5O2 = 4NO + 6H2O

Let us calculate how many moles of NH3 are in 51 g.

The mass of one mole of NH3 is 14 + 3 = 17 g.

17 g is 1 mole.

51 g is X moles.

X = 5I g * I mole / I7 g = 3 moles.
From the equation, 4 moles of NH3 require 5 moles of O2.

3 moles of NH3 require X moles of O2.
X = 3 moles * 5 moles / 4 moles =3.75 moles.
I mole of O2 occupies 22.4 L.
3.75 moles of O2 occupy X L.
X = 3.75 mole * 22.4 L / I mole = 84 L.
Answer: 84 L of O2 is required to completely react with 51 g of NH3

19. Calculate the mass of silver nitrate in grams required to completely react with 7 moles of lead?

Pb +2AgNO3 -> Pb(NO3)2 +2Ag

The mass of one mole of AgNO3 is I08 + I4 +48=I70 g.
From the equation, one mole of Pb requires 2 moles of AgNO3.
Seven moles of Pb require X moles of AgNO3.
X = 7 moles * 2 moles/I mole = I4 mole of AgNO3.
I mole of AgNO3 is I70 g.
I4 moles of AgNO3 is X g.
X = I4 moles * I70 g/I mole =2380 g.
Answer: 2380 g of AgNO3 is required to completely react with 7 moles of Pb.

20. Calculate the mass of carbon in grams that must react with Oxygen to produce 12x10^23 molecules of Carbon Dioxide.

(CO2) C + O2 = CO2

One mole of any substance contains Avogadro number of particles, and it is 6.022*10^23 per gram mol.
We have I2*I0^23 of CO2. It is approximately 2 moles of CO2.
The mass of one mole of CO2 is I2 + 32=44 g.
The mass of 2 moles of CO2 is 88 g.
The mass of one mole of C is I2 g.

From the equation, one mole of C produces one mole of CO2.

12 g C produces 44 g of CO2.

X g C produces 88 g of CO2.

X = 12 g * 88 g / 44 g = 24 g C.

Answer: 24 g of C is required to produce 12*10^23 molecules of CO2

21. How many liters of hydrogen gas are required to completely hydrogenate 952 g of 2-butene?

CH3-CH=CH-CH3 + H2 = CH3-CH2-CH2-CH3

Let us calculate how many moles of CH3-CH=CH-CH3 we have.

The mass of one mole of CH3-CH=CH-CH3 is 12 + 3 + 12 +1 + 12 + 1 + 12 +3=56 g.

1 mole is 56 g.

X moles is 952 g.

X = 1 mole * 952 g/ 56 g = 17 moles.

From the equation, one mole of H2 requires one mole of CH3-CH=CH-CH3.

X moles of H2 requires 17 moles of CH3-CH=CH-CH3.

X = 1 mole * 17 mole / 1 mole = 17 moles of H2.

1 mole of H2 occupies 22.4 L.

17 moles of H2 occupy X L.

X = 17 mole * 22.4 L/ 1 mole = 380.8 L.

Answer: 380.8 L of H2 is required to completely hydrogenate 952 g of CH3-CH=CH-CH3.

22. How many grams of barium chloride is required to completely precipitate barium sulfate from 1 liter of 0.3M H2SO4?

H2SO4 + BaCl2 -= BaSO4 + 2HCl

Let us calculate how many grams of H2SO4 we have.

The mass of one mole of H2SO4 is 98 g.

1 L of 1 M solution contains 98 g of H2SO4.

1 L of 0.3 M solution contains X g of H2SO4.

X =0.3M * 98 g/1 M = 29.4 g of H2SO4.

The mass of one mole of BaCl2 is 137 + 35*2 = 207 g.

From the equation, one mole of H2SO4 reacts with one mole of BaCl2.

98 g H2SO4 require 207 g of BaCl2.

29.4 g of H2SO4 require X g of BaCl2.

X = 29.4 g * 207 g / 98 g = 62.1 g BaCl2.

Answer: 62.1 g of BaCl2 is required to completely precipitate BaSO4 from 1 L of 0.3M H2SO4

23. What mass of potassium hydroxide is required to react completely with 1 liter of 0.1M sulfuric acid solution to produce potassium sulfate?

How many grams of K2SO4 will be produced?

2KOH + H2SO4 →2H2O + K2SO4

Let us calculate how many grams of H2SO4 we have.

The mass of one mole of H2SO4 is 98 g

1 L of 1M solution contains 98 g of H2SO4.

1 L of 0.1 M solution contains X g of H2SO4.

X = 0.1 M * 98 g / 1 M = 9.8 g.

From the equation, 2 moles of KOH react with one mole of H2SO4.

The mass of one mole of KOH is 39 + 17 = 56 g,

Then 2 moles of KOH is 112g.

112 g of KOH requires 98 g of H2SO4.

X g of KOH requires 9.8 g of H2SO4.

X = 112g * 9.8g /98 g = 11.2 g KOH

How many grams of K2SO4 are produced?

The mass of one mole of K2SO4 is 39 + 39 + 32 +64=174 g.

From the equation, one mole of H2SO4 produces one mole of K2SO4.

98 g H2SO4 produces 174 g of K2SO4.

9.8 g H2SO4 produces X g K2SO4.

X = 9.8 g * 174 g / 98 g = 17.4 g K2SO4

Answer: 11.2 g KOH is required to completely react with 1 L of 0.1 M H2SO4.

17.4 g of K2SO4 is produced.

24. What volume of 0.2M NaOH solution is required to completely neutralize 50.0 mL of 0.3M HCl solution?

NaOH + HCl = NaCl + H2O

From the equation, one mole of NaOH neutralizes one mole of HCl.

How many moles of HCl are in 50 ml 0.3 M solution?

1 L of 1 M solution contains 1 mole of HCl.

0.05 L of 1 M solution contains X mole of HCl.

X = 0.05 L * 1 mole/ 1 L = 0.05 moles.

0.05 L of 1 M solution contains 0.05 moles

0.05 L of 0.3 moles solution contains X moles.

X = 0.3 M * 0.05 moles/1M = 0.015 moles HC

50.0 mL of 0.3 M solution contains 0.015 moles of HCl.

1 L of 1 M NaOH solution contains 1 mole of NaOH.

1 L of 0.2 M solution contains X moles of NaOH.

X = 0.2 M * 1 mole/1M = 0.2 moles.

We need only 0.015 moles of NaOH. How many ml of NaOH solution do we need?

1 L of 0.2 M solution contains 0.2 moles.

X L of 0.2 M solution contains 0.015 moles.

X = 1 L * 0.015 moles/ 0.2 mole = 0.075 L

Answer: 0.075 L (75mL) of NaOH is required to completely neutralize 50.0 mL of 0.3M HCl

25. How many grams of MgCl2 are produced if 0.5 L of 0.5 M solution of HCL reacts with Mg(OH)2. How much Mg(OH)2 is spent?

Mg(OH)2 + 2HCl = MgCl2 + 2H2O

Let us calculate how much HCl we have in grams.

The mass of one mole of HCl is 36g.

1 L of 1 M solution contains 36 g of HCl.

1 L of 0.5 M solutions contain X g of HCl.

X = 0.5 M * 36 g / 1M = 18 g HCl.

1 L contains 18 g of HCl.

0.5 L contains X g of HCl.

X = 0.5 L * 18 g / 1L = 9 g of HCl.

The mass of one mole of MgCl2 is 24 + 70 = 94 g.

From the equation, two moles of HCl produce 1 mole of MgCl2.

36*2=72 g of HCl produces 94 g of MgCl2. We have only 9 g of HCl.

9 g of HCl produces X g of MgCl2.

X = 9 g * 94 g / 72 g = 11.75 g of MgCl2.

How much Mg(OH)2 is spent?

The mass of one mole of Mg(OH)2 is 24 + 17*2=58 g.

From the equation, 1 mole of Mg(OH)2 produces 1 mole of MgCl2.

58 g of Mg(OH)2 produce 94 g of MgCl2.

X g of Mg(OH)2 produce 11.75 g of MgCl2.

X = 58 g * 11.75 g / 94 g = 7.25 g of Mg(OH)2.

Answer: 11.75 g of MgCl2 is produced if 0.5 L of 0.5 M solution of HCL reacts with Mg(OH)2. 7.25 grams of Mg(OH)2 are spent.

26. How many grams of KClO3 would be required to produce 3 liters of O2? How many grams of KCl are produced?

2KClO3 = 3O2 + 2KCl

Let us calculate how much O2 we have in grams.

The mass of one mole of O2 is 32g.

One mole of gas occupies 22.4 L.

32 g occupy 22.4 L.

X grams occupy 3 L.

X = 32 g * 3 L / 22.4 L = 4.29 g of O2

The mass of one mole of KClO3 is 39 + 35 + 48 =122 g of KClO3.

The mass of one mole of KCl is 39 + 35 = 74 g of KCl.

From the equation, 2 moles of KClO3 produce 3 moles of O2 and 2 moles of KCl.

122*2=244 g of KClO3 produce 32*3=96 g of O2.

X grams of KClO3 produce 4.29 g of O2.

X = 244 g * 4.29 g / 96g = 10.9 g of KClO3 is required.

How many grams of KCl are produced?

From the equation, 2 moles of KClO3 produce 2 moles of KCl.

244 grams of KClO3 produce 148 g of KCl.

10.9 grams of KClO3 produce X g of KCl.

X = 10.9 g * 148 g/244g = 13.2 g of KCl.

Answer: 21.8 g of KClO3 is required to produce 3 L of O2. 13.2 grams of KCl are produced.

27. How many liters of 0.5M solution of HCl are required to completely react with 25.0 g of Aluminum? How many liters of H2 are produced?

2Al + 6 HCl =2AlCl3 + 3H2

Calculate how much HCl is in 1 L of 0.5 M solution.

The mass of one mole of HCl is 35+1=36 g.

1 L of 1M solution contains 36 g of HCl.

1 L of 0.5 M solution contains X g of HCl.

X = 0.5 M * 36 g / 1 M = 18 g per liter.

The mass of one mole of Al is 27 g.

From the equation, 2 moles of Al react with 6 moles of HCl.

27*2=54 grams of Al require 6*36=216 g of HCl.

25 grams of Al require X g of HCl.

X = 25g * 216 g /54 g = 100g HCl is required.

1 L of 0.5 M solution contains 18 g of HCl.

X L of 0.5 M solution contains 100g of HCl

X = 1 L * 100 g / 18 g = 5.6 L of HCl is required to completely react with 25 g of Al.

How many liters of H2 are produced?

From the equation, 2 moles of Al produce 3 moles of H2.

We have 25 g of Al. How many moles of Al do we have?

27 g is 1 mole.

25 g is X moles. X= 25 g * 1 mole/27 g = 0.93 moles.
Two moles of Al produce 3 moles of H2.
0.93 moles of Al produce X moles of H2.
X = 0.93 moles * 3 moles/2 moles = 1.39 moles of H2.

One mole of H2 occupies 22.4 L.
1.39 moles of H2 occupy X L.
X = 1.39 mole * 22.4 L /1 mole = 31.1 L.

Answer: 5.6 L of HCl are required to completely react with 25 g of Al.

31.1 L of H2 are produced.

28. How many grams of Nitrogen would be required to completely react with 11.2 liters of hydrogen to produce ammonia? How many grams of ammonia are produced?

N2 + 3 H2 = 2 NH3

Let us calculate how many grams of H2 we have.
The mass of one mole of H2 is 2 g.
1 mole of H2 occupies 22.4 L.
2 g of H2 occupies 22.4 L.
X g of H2 occupies 11.2 L.
X = 2 g * 11.2 L / 22.4 L = 1 g.
The mass of one mole of N2 is 14*2=28 g
The mass of one mole of NH3 is 14+3=17 g
From the equation, one mole of N2 reacts with 3 moles of H2, producing 2 moles of NH3.
28 g of N2 react with 6 g of H2.
X g of N2 react with 1 g of H2.
X = 28 g * 1 g / 6 g = 4.7 g of N2 are required for 11.2 L (1 g) of H2.
How many grams of ammonia are produced? From the equation, one mole of N2 produces 2 moles of NH3.
28 g of N2 produce 17*2=34 g of NH3.
4.7 g of N2 produce X g of NH3.

X = 4.7 g * 34 g /28 g = 5.7 g of NH3.

Answer: 4.7 g of N2 are required to completely react with 11.2 L (1 g) of H2. 5.7 grams of NH3 are produced.

29. Calculate the volume of 0.5 M sulfuric acid solution in milliliters required to completely neutralize 100 ml of 1 M solution of KOH?

H2SO4 + 2KOH = K2SO4 + 2H2O

What is the K+ ion concentration at the end of the reaction?
Let us calculate how many moles of H2SO4 are in I L of 0.5 M solution.
I L of I M solution of H2SO4 contains I mole.
I L of 0.5 M solution contains X moles.
X = 0.5 M * I mole / I M = 0.5 moles.

How many moles of KOH do we have?
I L of I M solution of KOH contains I mole.
0.I L of IM solution of KOH contains X moles.
X = 0.I L * I mole / I L = 0.I mole of KOH.
From the equation, I mole of H2SO4 reacts with 2 moles of KOH.
X moles of H2SO4 react with 0.I moles of KOH.
X = I mole * 0.I moles / 2 moles = 0.05 moles of H2SO4 is required.
I L of 0.5 M solution of H2SO4 contains 0.5 moles.
X L of 0.5 M solution of H2SO4 contains 0.05 moles.
X = I L * 0.05 moles / 0.5 moles = 0.I L = 100 mL of 0.5 M H2SO4 is required.
What is the K+ ion concentration at the end of the reaction?
We calculated above that we initially had 0.I moles of KOH in a 100 ml solution.
Then we added 100 mL of H2SO4. The total volume becomes 100ml + 100 ml = 200 ml.
Initially, we had 0.I moles of KOH.
What is K+ concentration in M if we have 0.I moles per 200 ml?
0.I mole per 200 ml.
X mole per I L

66

X = 0.1 moles * 1 L / 0.2 L = 0.5 moles per 1 Liter or 0.5 M.
Answer: 100 mL of 0.5 M H2SO4 is required to neutralize 100 mL of 1 M solution of KOH. The K+ concentration at the end of the reaction is 0.5 M.

30. How many grams of Fe2O3 are required to completely react with 3 moles of Al?

2Al + Fe2O3 = 2Fe + Al2O3

The mass of one mole of Fe2O3 is 56 * 2 + 16*3 = 160g.

The mass of one mole of Al is 27g.
From the equation, 2 moles of Al react with one mole of Fe2O3.
54 g of Al (2 moles) react with 160 g of Fe2O3.
81 g of Al (3 moles) react with X g of Fe2O3.
X = 81 g * 160 g /54 g = 240 g of Fe2O3.

Answer: 240 grams of Fe2O3 are required to completely react with 3 moles of Al.

31. How much Copper is produced if 200 ml of 1M CuSO4 solution reacts with 26 g of iron powder?

CuSO4 + Fe = FeSO4 + Cu.

Solution: The mass of one mole of CuSO4 is 64 + 32 + 16*4 = 160g. How did we get it?

The mass of Cu is 64, the mass of S is 32, and the mass of O is 16. (16*4=64)
An 1M solution of CuSO4 has one mole per liter. It means one liter of CuSO4 contains 98 g of H2SO4.
We have 200 ml of CuSO4. How many grams of CuSO4 in 200 ml?
1000 ml is 160g of CuSO4.
200 ml is X g of CuSO4.
X = 200ml * 160g/ 1000ml = 32 g of CuSO4.
The mass of Cu is 64. One mole of Cu is 64 g.
This equation shows that one mole of CuSO4 produces one mole of Cu.

160 g of $CuSO_4$ produce 64 g of Cu.

32 g of $CuSO_4$ produce X gram of Cu.

X = 32g * 64g / 160g =12.8 g of Cu,

If we have enough Fe, 32 g of $CuSO_4$ can produce 12.8 g of Cu.

Do we have enough Fe to react completely with 32 g of H_2SO_4?

The mass of Fe is 56. One mole of Fe weighs 56g.

The equation shows that one mole of H_2SO_4 requires one mole of Fe.

160 g of $CuSO_4$ requires 56 g of Fe,

We have 32 g of $CuSO_4$. How many grams of Fe do we need for a complete reaction?

160 g $CuSO_4$ require 56g Fe.

32g $CuSO_4$ require X g Fe.

X = 32 * 56 / 160 = 11.2 g of Fe is required.

We have 26 g of Fe. Not all Fe will react with 32g of H_2SO_4.

How much Fe will be left?

26g of Fe – 11.2g of Fe = 14.8 g of Fe is left.

Answer: 12.8 g of Cu is produced. 14.8 g of Fe is left.

32. How much KCl is produced if 70g of K reacts with 10 liters of Cl2?

Which initial reactant will be left over? 2K + Cl2 = 2KCl

First, we must determine which reactant is limited and which will be left over. The equation shows that 2 moles of K react with one mole of Cl2.

K atomic mass = 39.0983 grams or we can round it to 39.1g.

2 moles of K is 39.1*2=78.2g. One mole of Cl2 is 35*2=70g.

78.2g of K reacts with 70g of Cl2.

How many g of Cl2 do we have?

One mole of gas is 22.4L. It means:

70g of Cl2 is 22.4 L.

X g of Cl2 is 10 L.

X = 70 * 10 / 22.4 = 31.25g. 10 L of Cl2 is 31.25g.

2 moles of K react with one mole of Cl2.

We have 70 g of K. How much Cl2 is required in grams?

78.2g of K react with 70 g of Cl2

70 g of K reacts with X g of Cl2.

X = 70g * 70 g /78.2g = 62.7 g of Cl2.

We need 62.7 g of Cl2 per reaction, but we have only 31.25g. It means Cl2 is limited, and K will be left over. We have to use the limited reactant, Cl2, to calculate how much KCl is produced.

The equation shows that one mole of Cl2 produces 2 moles of KCl.

One mole of Cl2 is 35*2=70 g.

Two moles of KCl is (39.1 + 35) * 2=**148.2g.**

One mole of Cl2 produces 2 moles of KCl.

70g of Cl2 produces **148.2g** of KCl.

31.25g of Cl2 produces X g of KCl.

X = 31.25 * 148.2 / 70 =66.16 g of KCl.

Answer: 66.16 g of KCl is produced. K will be left over.

33. How many grams of K2SO4 are produced if 1 liter of 1M KOH reacts with 1 Liter of 0.5 M H2SO4? Which initial reactant will be left over?

2KOH + H2SO4 = K2SO4 + 2H2O.

First, let us calculate how many grams of KOH and H2SO4 we have. Then determine which reactant is limited.

The mass of one mole of KOH is 39.1 + 16 + 1=56.1g.

1 liter of 1M of KOH contains 56.1g of KOH.

The mass of one mole of H2SO4 is 2 + 32 + 16*4 ≈ 98g.

1 liter of 1M solution of H2SO4 contains 98g H2SO4.

We have a 0.5M solution of H2SO4.

1 L of 1 M of H2SO4 contains 98g.

1 L of 0.5M of H2SO4 contains X g.

X=0.5 * 98 / 1 = 49g. H2SO4.

 The equation shows that two moles of KOH react with one mole of H2SO4.

One mole of KOH is 56.1g, 2 moles are 112.2g.

112.2g of KOH reacts with 98g of H2SO4.

56.1g of KOH reacts with X g of H2SO4.

X = 56.1g * 98g /112.2g = 49g H2SO4.

We found that for an existing amount of KOH (56.1g), we need 49 g of H2SO4.

Since 1 L of 0.5M solution of H2SO4 contains 49g H2SO4, we have enough H2SO4 for a complete reaction with the existing amount of KOH. No reactant is left over. We can use either one to calculate how much K2SO4 will be produced. Let us use KOH.

The mass of one mole of K2SO4 is 39.1*2 + 32 + 16*4= 174.2g.

From the equation, we see that 2 mole of KOH produces one mole of K2SO4.

112.2g KOH produces 174.2g of K2SO4.

56.1g KOH produce X g K2SO4.

X = 56.1 * 174.2 /112.2 = 87g.

Answer: 87 g of K2SO4 is produced. No reactant is left.

34. How many grams of K2SO4 is produced if 0.1 liter of 0.1M solution of KOH reacts with 0.1 Liter of 0.1 M solution of H2SO4? Which initial reactant will be left over?

H2SO4 + 2KOH = K2SO4 + 2H2O

Let us calculate how much KOH and H2SO4 we have in grams.

Mass of one mole of KOH is 39 + 16 + 1 = 56g

1 L of 1M solution of KOH contains 56g of KOH.

1 L of 1 M of KOH - 56 g

1 L of 0.1M of KOH - X g

X = 56 g * 0.1 M/1 M = 5.6g of KOH

Then 1 L of 0.1 M solution will contain 5.6 g KOH.

We have 0.1 L of KOH solution.

1 L of KOH - 5.6 g

0.1 L of KOH - X g

X = 0.1L * 5.6g / 1 L= 0.56 g KOH.

The mass of H2SO4 is 2 + 32 + 16*4=98 g.

I L of I M of H_2SO_4 solution contains 98 g.

I L of 0.I M of H_2SO_4 solution contains X g.

X = 0.I * 98 /I = 0.98 g of H_2SO_4.

I L of 0.I M solution contains 9.8 g H_2SO_4.

0.I L of 0.I M solution contains X g.

X= 0.I * 9.8 / I = 0.98 g. We have 0.98 g of H_2SO_4.

We have 0.56 g of KOH and 0.98 g of H_2SO_4. Which reactant is limited?

From our equation, 2 mole of KOH reacts with one mole of H_2SO_4.

56 * 2 = II2 g KOH reacts with 98 g of H_2SO_4.

0.56 g of KOH reacts with X g of H_2SO_4.

X = 0.56g * 98 g / II2 g = 0.49 g H_2SO_4.

For 0.56 g KOH, we need 0.49 g H_2SO_4, and we have 0.98 g H_2SO_4.

It means that H_2SO_4 will be left over.

KOH is a limited reactant, and we have to use KOH to calculate how much K_2SO_4 is produced.

The mass of one mole of K_2SO_4 is 39*2 + 32 + 64 = 174 g.

Two moles of KOH produce one mole of K_2SO_4.

II2 g KOH produces 174g K_2SO_4.

0.56 g KOH produce X g K_2SO_4.

X = 0.56 g * 174 g /II2 g = 0.87 g K_2SO_4.

Answer: KOH is a limited reactant. 0.87 g of K_2SO_4 is produced.

35. How many grams of $Ba(NO_3)_2$ are produced if 0.1 liter of 0.1 M solution of HNO_3 reacts with 0.1 liter of 0.1 M solution of $Ba(OH)_2$? Which initial reactant will be left over?

$2HNO_3 + Ba(OH)_2 = Ba(NO_3)_2 + 2H_2O$.

Let us calculate how much HNO_3 and $Ba(OH)_2$ we have in grams.

The mass of one mole of HNO_3 is I + 14 +16*3= 63 g

I L of IM solution of HNO_3 contains 63 g.

0.I L of I M solution of HNO_3 contains X g.

X = 0.1 * 63 /1 = 6.3 g of HNO3.

0.1 L of 1 M solution of HNO3 contains 6.3 g.

0.1 L of 0.1 M solution of HNO3 contains X g.

X = 0.1 M * 6.3 g /1 M= 0.63 g.

So, we have 0.63 g of HNO3.

The mass of one mole of Ba(OH)2 = 137 + 2 * (16 + 1) = 171 g.

1 L of 1 M solution of Ba(OH)2 contains 171 g.

1 L of 0.1 M solution of Ba(OH)2 contains X g.

X = 0.1 M * 171 g /1 M = 17.1 g.

1 L of 0.1 M solution of Ba(OH)2 contains 17.1 g.

0.1 L of 0.1 M solution of Ba(OH)2 contains X g.

X = 0.1 L * 17.1 g/ 1 L = 1.71 g.

So, we have 1.17 g of Ba(OH)2 and 0.63 g of HNO3. Which reactant is limited, and which will be left over?

The equation shows that 2 moles of HNO3 react with one mole of Ba(OH)2.

One mole of HNO3 is 63 g. Two moles are 63 * 2 = 126 g.

One mole of Ba(OH)2 is 171 g.

126 g of HNO3 react with 171 g of Ba(OH)2.

0.63 g of HNO3 react with X g of Ba(OH)2.

X = 0.63g * 171g / 126g = 0.85 g Ba(OH)2.

This reactant will be left over since we have 17.1 g of Ba(OH)2 and need only 0.85g of Ba(OH)2.

We should use HNO3 to calculate how much Ba(NO3)2 is produced.

The mass of one mole of Ba(NO3)2 is 137 + 2(14 + 15*3) = 137 + 2 (14 + 48) = 261 g.

Two moles of HNO3 produce one mole of Ba(NO3)2.

One mole of HNO3 contains 63 g. Two moles are equal to 126g.

126 g of HNO3 produces 261 g Ba(NO3)2.

0.63 g of HNO3 produce X g of Ba(NO3)2.

X = 0.63 * 261 /126 = 1.3 g of Ba(NO3)2.

Answer: 1.3 g of Ba(NO3)2 is produced. HNO3 is a limited reactant. Ba (OH)2 will be left over.

36. How many liters of 0.1M solutions of NaOH are required to produce 1 liters of 0.1M solution of Na3PO4 in the following reaction:

H3PO4 + 3NaOH = Na3PO4 + 3H2O

How many moles of H3PO4 will be spent?

First, calculate how many grams in 1 L of 0.5M solution of Na3PO4.

The mass of one mole of Na3PO4 is 23 * 3 + 31 + 16*4 = 164 g.

1 L of 1M solution of Na3PO4 contains 164 g of Na3PO4.

1 L of 0.1 M solution of Na3PO4 contains X g of Na3PO4.

X = 0.1 M * 164g / 1 M = 16.4 g of Na3PO4.

So, 16.4 g of Na3PO4 is produced.

How many grams of NaOH do we need for that?

From the equation, 3 moles of NaOH are required to produce one mole of Na3PO4.

The mass of one mole of NaOH is 23 + 16 + 1 = 40 g. 3 moles are 40 * 3 = 120g.

120 grams of NaOH produce 164 g of Na3PO4.

X g of NaOH produces 16.4 g of Na3PO4.

X= 120 g * 16.4 g /164 g = 12 g.

We need 12 g of NaOH to produce 16.4 g of Na3PO4.

Let us calculate how many grams of NaOH are in 1 L of 0.1 M solution of NaOH.

1 L of 1 M solution of NaOH contains 40 g of NaOH.

1 L 0.1 M solution of NaOH contains X g of NaOH.

X = 0.1 M * 40g / 1 L = 4g

Now we can calculate how many liters of 0.1 M solution of NaOH we need.

1 L contains 4 g NaOH.

X L contains 12 g NaOH.

X = 1 * 12 / 4 = 3 L.

Answer: 3 L of 0.1M solutions of NaOH are required to produce 1 liters of 0.1M solution of Na3PO4.

37. How many liters of H2 will be produced if 10 grams of Ca reacts with 1 liter of 0.1M solution of H2SO4? Which initial reactant will be left over?

Ca + H2SO4 = CaSO4 + H2

Let us calculate how much H2SO4 we have in grams.

The mass of one mole of H2SO4 is 2 + 32 + 64 = 98 g. H2SO4

I L of IM solution contains 98 g H2SO4. We have only 0.5 L

I M solution contains 98 g H2SO4.

0.I M solution contains X g H2SO4.

X = 0.I M * 98g/I M = 9.8 g H2SO4

So, I L of a 0.I M solution contains 9.8 g of H2SO4.

Let us calculate how much H2SO4 we need to completely react with 10 g of Ca

From the equation, one mole of Ca reacts with one mole of H2SO4.

The mass of one mole of Ca is 40 g.

40 g of Ca reacts with 98 g of H2SO4.

I0 g of Ca reacts with X g of H2SO4.

X = I0g * 98g / 40g =24.5 g of H2SO4.

We have 9.8 g of H2SO4, but we need 24.5 g. It means that H2SO4 is limited, and Ca will be left over.

To calculate how many liters of H2 are produced, we have to use H2SO4.

From the equation, one mole of H2SO4 produces one mole of H2, and one mole of H2 is 22.4 L

98 g of H2SO4 produce 22.4 L H2.

9.8 g of H2SO4 produce X L of H2.

X=9.8g * 22.4 L/ 98g = 2.24 L H2.

Answer: 2.24 L H2 is produced. Ca is left over.

38. How many grams of AgCl will be produced if 0.1 liter of 0.1M solution of AgNO3 reacts with 1 liter of 0.1M solution of CaCL2? Which initial reactant will be left over?

2AgNO3 + CaCl2 = 2AgCl + Ca(NO3)2

Let us calculate how much of each reactant we have in grams. Let us start with AgNO3.

The mass of one mole of AgNO3 is $108 + 14 + 48 = 170$ g.

1 L of 1M solution of AgNO3 contains 170g of AgNO3.

1 L of 0.1M solution contains X g of AgNO3.

X = 0.1M * 170g /1M=17 g of AgNO3.

Let us calculate how much CaCl2 we have in grams.

The mass of one mole of CaCl2 is $40 + 35*2=110$g.

1 L of 1M solution of CaCl2 contains 110g of CaCl2.

1 L of 0.1M solution contains X g of CaCl2.

X = 0.1M * 110g/1M = 11g of CaCl2.

1L of 0.1 M solution of CaCl2 contains 11g of CaCl2.

0.1 L of 0.1M solution of CaCl2 contains X g CaCl2.

X = 11g * 0.1L / 1L = 1.1g of CaCl2.

From the equation, 2 moles of AgNO3 react with one mole of CaCl2.

340g (170 *2) AgNO3 react with 110 g of CaCl2.

17 g AgNO3 reacts with X g CaCl2.

X = 17g * 110g /340g = 5.5 g CaCl2 is required.

Since 17 g of AgNO3 and 5.5 g of CaCl2 are required to complete the reaction, and we have 11g of CaCl2, CaCl2 will be left over. AgNO3 is a limited reactant, and we should use AgNO3 to calculate how much AgCl is produced.

The mass of one mole of AgCl is $108 + 35=143$ g.

From the equation, 2 moles of AgNO3 produce 2 moles of AgCl.

Two moles of AgNO3 equal 340g, and 2 moles of AgCl are equivalent to 286g.

340 g of AgNO3 produce 286 g AgCl.

17g of AgNO3 produce X g AgCl.

X = 17 * 286 /340 =14.3 g of AgCl.

Answer: 14.3 g of AgCl are produced. CaCl2 will be left over.

39. How many liters of 0.1 M solution of H2SO4 are

required to produce 5 g of ZnSO4? How many grams of Zn(OH)2 are spent?

Zn(OH)2 + H2SO4 = ZnSO4 + 2H2O

Let us calculate how much H2SO4 we have in I L of 0.I M solution in grams.

The mass of H2SO4 is 2 + 32 + 64 = 98 g.

I L of I M solution contains 98g of H2SO4.

I L of 0.I M solution contains X g of H2SO4.

X = 0.I M * 98g / IM = 9.8g of H2SO4.

The mass of one mole of ZnSO4 is 65 + 32 + 64 = I6I g

From the equation, one mole of H2SO4 produces one mole of ZnSO4.

98 g H2SO4 produce I6I g ZnSO4.

X g H2SO4 produces 5 g ZnSO4.

X = 98g * 5g /I6Ig = 3 g of H2SO4.

I L of 0.I M solution contains 9.8 g H2SO4.

X L of 0.I M solution contains 3g H2SO4.

X = I L * 3 g /9.8 g = 0.3 L H2SO4.

How many grams of Zn(OH)2 are spent?

The mass of one mole of Zn(OH)2 is I08 + (I6 + I)*2 = I42 g.

From the equation, one mole of Zn(OH)2 produces one mole of ZnSO4.

I42 g of Zn(OH)2 produce I6I g of ZnSO4.

X g of Zn(OH)2 produce 5 g of ZnSO4.

X = I42g * 5g / I6Ig =4.4 g of Zn(OH)2.

Answer: 0.3 L of 0.1 M solution of H2SO4 and 4.4 g of Zn(OH)2 are required to produce 5 g of ZnSO4.

40. How many grams of ZnSO4 are produced if 7 g of Zn(OH)2 react with 03L of 0.1M solution of H2SO4?

Zn(OH)2 + H2SO4 = ZnSO4 + 2H2O

Let us calculate how much H2SO4 we have in I L of 0.I M solution in grams.

The mass of H2SO4 is 2 + 32 + 64 = 98 g.

I L of I M solution contains 98g of H2SO4.

I L of 0.I M solution contains X g of H2SO4.

X = 0.I M * 98g / IM = 9.8g of H2SO4.

In I L of 0I.M solution, we have 9.8 g of H2SO2.

In 0.3L of 0.IM solution, we have X g of H2SO4.

X = 0.3L * 9.8g / I L = 2.94 g of H2SO4.

 Which reactant is limited, and which will be left over?

The mass of one mole of Zn(OH)2 is 108 + (16 + 1)*2 = 142 g.

From the equation, one mole of Zn(OH)2 produces one mole of ZnSO4.

142g of Zn(OH)2 react with 98g of H2SO4.

7g of Zn(OH)2 react with X g of H2SO4.

X = 7g * 98g / 142g = 4.8 g H2SO4.

We have only 2.94 g of H2SO4. It means that H2SO4 limited reactant and Zn(OH)2 will be left over.

We have to use H2SO4 to calculate how many grams of ZnSO4 is produced.

One mole of H2SO4 produces one mole of ZnSO4.

The mass of one mole of ZnSO4 is 65 + 32 + 64 = 161 g

The mass of one mole of H2SO4 is 98 g.

98 g of H2SO4 produce 161 g of ZnSO4

2.94 g of H2SO4 produce X g of ZnSO4

X = 2.94 g * 161 g / 98 g = 4.83 g of ZnSO4.

Answer: 7 g of Zn(OH)2 and 03L of 0.1M solution of H2SO4 produce 4.83 g of ZnSO4. Zn(OH)2 will be left over.

41. What mass of Sodium hydroxide is required to react completely with 0.5 liters of 0.5M sulfuric acid solution to produce Sodium sulfate? How many grams of Na2SO4 will be produced?

2NaOH + H2SO4 →2H2O + Na2SO4

Let us calculate how many grams of H2SO4 we have.

The mass of one mole of H2SO4 is 98 g

I L of IM solution contains 98 g of H2SO4.

I L of 0.5 M solution contains X g of H2SO4.

X = 0.5 M * 98 g / I M = 49 g of H2SO4.

We have 0.5 L of H2SO4.

I L of 0.5M H2SO4 contains 49g

0.5 L contains Xg of H2SO4

X = 0.5L * 49g / IL = 24.5g of H2SO4.

From the equation, 2 moles of NaOH react with one mole of H2SO4.

The mass of one mole of NaOH is 23 + 17 = 40 g,

Then 2 moles of NaOH is 80g.

80 g of NaOH requires 98 g of H2SO4.

X g of NaOH requires 24.5 g of H2SO4.

X = 80g * 24.5g /98 g = 20 g NaOH

How many grams of Na2SO4 are produced?

The mass of one mole of Na2SO4 is 46 + 32 +64=142 g.

From the equation, one mole of H2SO4 produces one mole of Na2SO4.

98 g H2SO4 produces 142 g of Na2SO4.

24.5 g H2SO4 produces X g Na2SO4.

X = 24.5 g * 142 g / 98 g = 35.5 g NA2SO4

Answer: 20 g NaOH is required to completely react with 0.5 L of 0.5 M H2SO4.

35.5 g of NA2SO4 is produced.

42. What volume of 0.1M Ca(OH)2 solution is required to completely neutralize 5.0 mL of 0.3M HCl solution?

Ca(OH)2 + 2HCl = CaCl2 + 2H2O

From the equation, one mole of Ca(OH)2 neutralizes two moles of HCl.

How many moles of HCl are in 5 ml 0.3 M solution?

5 ml = 0.005 L

I L of I M solution contains I mole of HCl.

0.005 L of I M solution contains X mole of HCl.

X = 0.005 L * I mole/ I L = 0.005 moles.

0.005 L of I M solution contains 0.005 moles.

0.005 L of 0.3 moles solution contains X moles.

X = 0.3 M * 0.005 moles/IM = 0.0015 moles HCl

5.0 mL of 0.3 M solution contains 0.0015 moles of HCl.

I L of I M Ca(OH)2 solution contains I mole of Ca(OH)2.

I L of 0.I M solution contains X moles of Ca(OH)2.

X = 0.I M * I mole/IM = 0.I moles.

Since one mole of Ca(OH)2 is required for two moles of HCl, and we have only 0.0015 moles of HCl, then we need only 0.0015/2 moles of Ca(OH)2.

0.0015 / 2 = 0.00075 moles of Ca(OH)2

How many L of Ca(OH)2 solution do we need?

I L of 0.I M solution contains 0.I moles.

X L of 0.I M solution contains 0.00075 moles of Ca(OH)2

X = I L * 0.00075 moles/ 0.I mole = 0.0075 L

Answer: 0.0075 L (7.5mL) of 0.1M solution of Ca(OH)2 is required to completely neutralize 5.0 mL of 0.3M solution of HCl

43. How many grams of MgCl2 are produced if 0.1 L of 0.1 M solution of HCL reacts with Mg(OH)2. How much Mg(OH)2 is spent?

Mg(OH)2 + 2HCl = MgCl2 + 2H2O

Let us calculate how much HCl we have in grams.

The mass of one mole of HCl is 36g.

I L of I M solution contains 36 g of HCl.

I L of 0.I M solutions contain X g of HCl.

X = 0.I M * 36 g / IM = 3.6 g HCl.

I L contains 33.6 g of HCl.

0.I L contains X g of HCl.

X = 0.I L * 3.6 g / IL = 0.36 g of HCl.

The mass of one mole of MgCl2 is 24 + 70 = 94 g.

From the equation, two moles of HCl produce I mole of MgCl2.

36*2 = 72 g of HCl produces 94 g of MgCl2. We have only 0.36 g of HCl.

0.36 g of HCl produces X g of MgCl2.

X = 0.36 g * 94 g / 72 g = 0.47 g of MgCl2.

How much Mg(OH)2 is spent?

The mass of one mole of Mg(OH)2 is 24 + 17*2=58 g.

From the equation, 1 mole of Mg(OH)2 produces 1 mole of MgCl2.

58 g of Mg(OH)2 produce 94 g of MgCl2.

X g of Mg(OH)2 produce 0.47 g of MgCl2.

X = 58 g * 0.47 g / 94 g = 0.29 g of Mg(OH)2.

Answer: 0.47 g of MgCl2 is produced if 0.1 L of 0.1 M solution of HCL reacts with Mg(OH)2. 0.29 grams of Mg(OH)2 are spent.

44. How many grams of KClO3 would be required to produce 22.4 liters of O2? How many grams of KCl are produced?

2KClO3 = 3O2 + 2KCl

Let us calculate how much O2 we have to produce in grams.

One mole of gas occupies 22.4 L

The mass of one mole of O2 is 32g. It means we need to produce 32g of O2.

The mass of one mole of KClO3 is 39 + 35 + 48 =122 g of KClO3.

The mass of one mole of KCl is 39 + 35 = 74 g of KCl.

From the equation, 2 moles of KClO3 produce 3 moles of O2 and 2 moles of KCl.

122*2=244 g of KClO3 produce 32*3=96 g of O2.

X grams of KClO3 produce 32 g of O2.

X = 244 g * 32 g / 96g = 81.3 g of KClO3 is required.

How many grams of KCl are produced?

From the equation, 2 moles of KClO3 produce 2 moles of KCl.

244 grams of KClO3 produce 148 g of KCl.

81.3 grams of KClO3 produce X g of KCl.

X = 81.3g * 148 g/244g = 49.3 g of KCl.

Answer: 81.3 g of KClO3 is required to produce 22.4 L of O2.

49.3 grams of KCl are produced.

45. How many liters of 0.1M solution of HCl is required to completely react with 5.0 g of Aluminum? How many liters of H2 are produced?

2Al + 6 HCl =2AlCl3 + 3H2

Calculate how much HCl is in 1 L of O.1 M solution.

The mass of one mole of HCl is 35+1=36 g.

1 L of 1M solution contains 36 g of HCl.

1 L of 0.1 M solution contains X g of HCl.

X = 0.1 M * 36 g / 1 M = 3.6 g per liter.

The mass of one mole of Al is 27 g.

From the equation, 2 moles of Al react with 6 moles of HCl.

27*2=54 grams of Al require 6*36=216 g of HCl.

5 grams of Al require X g of HCl.

X = 5g * 216 g /54 g = 20g HCl is required.

1 L of 0.1 M solution contains 3.6 g of HCl.

X L of 0.1 M solution contains 20g of HCl

X = 1 L * 20 g / 3.6 g = 5.6 L of HCl is required to completely react with 5 g of Al.

How many liters of H2 are produced?

From the equation, 2 moles of Al produce 3 moles of H2.

We have 5 g of Al. How many moles of Al do we have?

27 g is 1 mole.

5 g is X moles. X= 5 g * 1 mole/27 g = 0.19 moles.

Two moles of Al produce 3 moles of H2.

0.19 moles of Al produce X moles of H2.

X = 0.19 moles * 3 moles/2 moles = 0.285 moles of H2.

One mole of H2 occupies 22.4 L.

0.285 moles of H2 occupy X L.

X = 0.285 mole * 22.4 L /1 mole = 6.3 L.

Answer: 5.6 L of HCl is required to react completely with 5 g of Al. 6.3 L of H2 is produced.

46. How many liters of Nitrogen would be required to completely react with 5.6 liters of hydrogen to produce ammonia? How many grams of ammonia are produced?

N2 + 3 H2 = 2 NH3

Let us calculate how many grams of H2 we have.

The mass of one mole of H2 is 2 g.

I mole of H2 occupies 22.4 L.

2 g of H2 occupies 22.4 L.

X g of H2 occupies 5.6 L.

X = 2 g * 5.6 L / 22.4 L = 0.5 g.

The mass of one mole of N2 is 14*2=28 g

The mass of one mole of NH3 is 14+3=17 g

From the equation, one mole of N2 reacts with 3 moles of H2, producing 2 moles of NH3.

28 g of N2 react with 6 g of H2.

X g of N2 reacts with 0.5 g of H2.

X = 28 g * 0.5 g / 6 g =2.3 g of N2 is required for 55.6 L (0.5 g) of H2.

How many grams of ammonia are produced? From the equation, one mole of N2 produces 2 moles of NH3.

28 g of N2 produce 17*2=34 g of NH3.

22.3 g of N2 produce X g of NH3.

X = 2.3 g * 34 g /28 g = 2.8 g of NH3.

Answer: 2.8 g of N2 is required to completely react with 5.6 L (0.5 g) of H2. 2.3 grams of NH3 are produced.

47. Calculate the volume of 0.1 M sulfuric acid solution in milliliters required to completely neutralize 100 ml of 0.1 M solution of KOH?

H2SO4 + 2KOH = K2SO4 + 2H2O

How many moles of KOH do we have?

1 L of 1 M solution of KOH contains 1 mole.

0.1 L of 1M solution of KOH contains X moles.

X = 0.1 L * 1 mole / 1 L = 0.1 mole of KOH.

1 M solution of KOH contains 0.1 moles of KOH.

0.1M solution contains X moles of KOH.

X = 0.1 moles * 0.1 M/ 1M = 0.01 moles of KOH.

From the equation, 1 mole of H_2SO_4 reacts with 2 moles of KOH.

X moles of H_2SO_4 react with 0.01 moles of KOH.

X = 1 mole * 0.01 moles / 2 moles = 0.005 moles of H_2SO_4 is required.

1L or 1000ml of 1M solution of H_2SO_4 contains 1 mole of it.

1L or 1000ml of 0.1M solution of H_2SO_4 contains X moles of it.

X = 0.1M * 1 mole /1M = 0.1 mole.

1000 ml contains 0.1 moles of H_2SO_4.

X ml contains 0.005 moles of H_2SO_4.

X = 1000ml * 0.005 moles / 0.1 moles = 50ml.

Answer: 50 mL of 0.1 M solution of H_2SO_4 is required to neutralize 100 mL of 0.1 M solution of KOH.

48. How many liters of NH_3 are required to produce 10 grams of NH_4HCO_3?

How many liters of CO_2 will be spent in the following reaction?

NH_3 + CO_2 + H_2O = NH_4HCO_3

In this problem, we calculate moles, and knowing that one mole of gas occupies 22.4 L, we can calculate liters.

Let's calculate the molecular mass of NH_4HCO_3.

N =14, 5H = 5, C = 12, 3O=48

The molecular mass of NH_4HCO_3 =14 + 5 + 12 + 48 = 79

How many moles of NH_4HCO_3 do we have in 10 grams?

79 g = 1 mole.

10 g = X moles.

X = 10g * 1 mole/79 g = 0.12 moles.

One mole of NH_3 produces one mole of NH_4HCO_3.

X moles of NH_3 produce 0.12 moles of NH_4HCO_3.

X = I mole * 0.12 moles /I mole = 0.12 moles NH3.

I mole of NH3 occupies 22.4 L.

0.12 mole of NH3 occupies X L.

X = 0.12 mole * 22.4 L /I mole = 2.69 L.

How many liters of CO2 are spent?

From the equation, one mole of CO2 produces one mole of NH4HCO3.

X moles of CO2 produce 0.12 moles of NH4HCO3.

X = 0.12 moles, and the volume is 2.69 L.

Answer: 2.69 L of NH3 and 2.69 L of CO2 are required to produce 10 grams of NH4HCO3.

49. How many liters of 0.1 M solution of H2SO4 are required to produce 5 g of Al2(SO4)3 and how many grams of Al(OH)3 are spent?

2Al(OH)3 + 3H2SO4 = Al2(SO4)3 + 6H2O

Let us calculate how much H2SO4 we have in grams in I L of 0.I M solution.

The mass of H2SO4 is 2 + 32 + 64 = 98 g.

I L of I M solution contains 98g of H2SO4.

I L of 0.I M solution contains X g of H2SO4.

X = 0.I M * 98g / IM = 9.8g.

The mass of one mole Al2(SO4)3 is 27*2 + (32 + 64) * 3 = 342 g.

From the equation, 3 moles of H2SO4 are required to produce one mole of Al2(SO4)3.

294 g (98 * 3) H2SO4 produce 342 g Al2(SO4)3.

X g H2SO4 produce 5 g Al2(SO4)3.

X = 5g * 294g /342g=4.3 g of H2SO4.

I L of 0.IM solution of H2SO4 contains 9.8 g of H2SO4.

X L of 0.I M solution of H2SO4 contains 4.3 g of H2SO4.

X = IL * 4.3 g/9.8 g = 0.44 L of 0.3 M solution of H2SO4.

How many grams of Al(OH)3 is spent?

The mass of one mole of Al(OH)3 is 27 + 17*3 = 78 g.

From the equation, 2 moles of Al(OH)3 are required to produce one Al2(SO4)3 mole.

156 g (2*78) of Al(OH)3 produce 342 g of Al2(SO4)3.

X g of Al(OH)3 produce 5 g of Al2(SO4)3.

X = 156 g * 5 g / 342 g = 2.28 g of Al(OH)3.

Answer: To produce 5 g of Al2(SO4)3, 0.44 L of 0.1M solution of H2SO4 and 2.28 g of Al(OH)3 are required.

50. How many grams of Al is required to produce 11.2 liters of H2 if Al reacts with 0.1M solutions of HCl? How many liters of solution of HCl will be spent?

2Al + 6HCl = 2AlCl3 + 3H2

Let us calculate how much Al is required to produce 11.2 L of H2.

The equation shows that 2 moles of Al produce 3 moles of H2.

2 moles of Al equals 27 * 2 = 54 g. 3 moles of H2 is equal to 3*22.4 L = 67.2 L.

56 g of Al produces 67.2 L of H2.

X g of Al produces 11.2 L H2.

X = 56 g * 11.2L /67.2 L = 9.3 g Al.

Now let us calculate how much HCl is required to produce 11.2 L of H2.

From the equation, 6 moles of HCL produce 3 moles of H2.

The mass of one mole of HCl is 1 + 35 = 36g. The mass of 6 moles is 36 g * 6 = 216 g.

As we calculated before, 3 moles of H2 occupy 67.2 L.

216 g of HCl produces 67.2 L H2.

X g of HCl produces 11.2 L of H2.

X = 216 g * 11.2 L/67.2 L = 36 g of HCl.

If 1 L of 1M solution of HCL is 36 g/L, then 1 L of 0.1 M solution is 3.6 g/L.

3.6 g of HCl is in 1 L of 0.1 M solution.

36g of HCl is in X L of 0.1 M solution.

X = 36 g * 1L/ 3.6 g = 10 L.

Answer: 9.3 g of Al and 10 L of 0.1 M solution of HCl are required to produce 11.2 L of H2

Dear Reader!

Thank you for reading my book! If you enjoyed this book or found it helpful, I'd be very grateful if you'd post a short review on Amazon. Your support does make a difference. Your feedback helps to improve this book.

Thanks again for your support!

Author's Books on Amazon.com

The Easiest Way to Understand Algebra: Algebra equations with answers and solutions.

Geometry For Students and Parents: Key concepts, problems, and solutions

Help Your Child with Homework: Algebra, Geometry, Chemistry

How to Create and Store Your Passwords: Hacker's Guide

The Ultimate eBook Creator: A Master Guide on How to Create, Design, and Format Your eBook Using Free Software

Creating Colorful Images with the PHP GD Library: Computer Programming for Fun by Examples

PHP Programming for Beginners: Key Programming Concepts. How to use PHP with MySQL and Oracle databases

C++ Programming by Examples: Key Computer Programming Concepts for Beginners

Learn SQL By Examples: Examples of SQL Queries and Stored Procedures for MySQL and Oracle Databases

Learn Critical Computer Programming Concepts: Three books in one with code examples and hands-on projects.

About The Author

Roy Richard Sawyer is currently living in Florida.
He obtained a master's degree in biology from a foreign University, where he specialized in neurophysiology.
He also has a degree in Computer Science from BMCC, which he attained after moving to the US.
Since then, Roy has been a software quality specialist and web developer for a computer company in Florida.
He has more than ten years of teaching experience and a long-standing interest in new computer technologies, psychology, and brain physiology.
When he has time to relax, Roy enjoys swimming in the Gulf of Mexico or walking with his dog on the Honeymoon Island Osprey Trail.

Printed in Great Britain
by Amazon

33879864R00056